"Once again, Dr. Al Mohler has written a book that shakes us up and challenges our thinking. *The Conviction to Lead* is poised to become one of the all-time classic works on Christian leadership."

Jim Daly, president, Focus on the Family

"Your character makes a difference every day. It provides the foundation for the work you do and instills confidence in the hearts of the people who look to you for leadership. Furthermore, true leadership, worthy of our heroic tradition, requires leaders to get results. When it is in our hands to do so, we must not fail to accomplish the good, to believe in the true, and to create the beautiful. Albert Mohler provides you with an excellent resource to develop your heart and mind in order to be prepared to lead with conviction."

Mike Huckabee, former governor of Arkansas;
host of Fox News Channel's *Huckabee* and nationally syndicated radio
program *The Mike Huckabee Show*; bestselling author

"Having rarely thought about leadership, I was hooked from the first chapter—to my complete surprise. This is a powerful book and gracefully written."

Fred Barnes, executive editor, *The Weekly Standard*

"Dr. Mohler stands in this generation as a rare example—a great leader who speaks with a clear voice. His sense of direction is anchored by deep, battle-tested convictions and applied with uncanny wisdom. We have been waiting to become students of his on this critical theme. With the arrival of this book, class is in session!"

John MacArthur, pastor of Grace Community Church,
Sun Valley, California; author of the *MacArthur Study Bible*

"I like how Al Mohler begins this book on leadership when he says, 'Convictions are not merely beliefs we hold; they are those beliefs that hold us.' Christians are called to lead by proclaiming the gospel message that not only convicts the sinner but holds us accountable to the Lordship of Jesus Christ. We must stand on the convictions that bolster our faith and lead us into spiritual battle with victory in sight. Stand firm, stand strong, and stand true to God's Word."

Franklin Graham, president and CEO, Samaritan's Purse, Billy Graham Evangelistic Association

"Barely can I tolerate books on leadership—but this one is fun, true, and written from the matrix of a life of one of the most distinctive Christian leaders of our era. Dr. Albert Mohler, in *The Conviction To Lead*, has captured the missing element in most discussions and in so doing paints a verbal canvass that will be forgotten by none who venture into these pages."

Paige Patterson, president, Southwestern Baptist Theological Seminary, Fort Worth, Texas

"Quintessential Albert Mohler! I am pleased to recommend *The Conviction to Lead*, which represents the reflective and purposeful path that has charted Dr. Mohler's twenty highly influential years of leadership at one of the truly fine institutions in the land. Convictional, challenging, insightful, and persuasive, this most important volume will certainly become a 'must read' for leaders, administrators, and board members, regardless of their spheres of service, for years to come."

David S. Dockery, president, Union University; general editor, *Christian Leadership Essentials*

THE
CONVICTION
TO LEAD

THE
CONVICTION
TO LEAD

25

PRINCIPLES
FOR LEADERSHIP
THAT MATTERS

ALBERT MOHLER

BETHANY HOUSE PUBLISHERS
a division of Baker Publishing Group
Minneapolis, Minnesota

© 2012 by R. Albert Mohler Jr.

Published by Bethany House Publishers
11400 Hampshire Avenue South
Bloomington, Minnesota 55438
www.bethanyhouse.com

Bethany House Publishers is a division of
Baker Publishing Group, Grand Rapids, Michigan

Printed in the United States of America

ISBN 978-0-7642-1125-6

The Library of Congress has catalogued the hardcover edition as follows:
Mohler, Albert.
      The conviction to lead : 25 principles for leadership that matters / Albert Mohler.
        p.   cm.
      Includes bibliographical references and index.
      Summary: "The president of an influential seminary and media personality reveals the characteristics of a true leader"—Provided by publisher.
      ISBN 978-0-7642-1004-4 (hardcover : alk. paper)
      ISBN 978-0-7642-1125-6 (pbk.)
      1. Leadership. 2. Christian leadership. I. Title.
BF637.L4M64 2012
158'.4—dc23   2012028750

Cover design by Lookout Design, Inc.
Cover photography by Robert H. Hoke III, Louisville, Kentucky

Author is represented by Wolgemuth and Associates

18   19   20   21   22   23   24   10 9 8 7 6 5 4

This book is lovingly dedicated to

MARY

Without whom the story would never be told,
And with whom the story is wonderful.

There are chapters yet to be written, and joys yet to be known.

*Enjoy life with the wife whom you love, all the days of your vain life
that he has given you under the sun, because that is your portion in
life and in your toil at which you toil under the sun.*
Ecclesiastes 9:9

Contents

Acknowledgments

No book is written alone. I undertook to write this book because my friends insisted that I write it, and they would give me no peace. C. J. Mahaney, along with Mark Dever and Ligon Duncan, pushed me to write this book. My agent and friend, Robert Wolgemuth, encouraged me (an understatement) to write this book, and convinced me that it was important enough to displace some other priorities. Other wise friends and colleagues pressed me to write it, and so I did.

I could not have written this book (or any other) without the constant encouragement of my wife, Mary, who read it chapter by chapter and offered invaluable counsel. More importantly, every day she inspires me to be a better leader and a more faithful man. Our children, Katie and Christopher, are always a part of everything we do and will forever be part of everything we are.

Southern Seminary colleagues Matt Hall, Jason Allen, and Dan Dumas read the chapters and contributed good advice. One of the greatest privileges of my life is to serve among some of the most outstanding leaders in the Christian world—those who serve with me on the Executive Cabinet at the Southern Baptist Theological Seminary. Each of them is an outstanding leader in his own right.

I taught a graduate course on leadership as the book was being written, and the class of bright young students served as lab rats for my developing manuscript. Thankfully, they received it enthusiastically.

My teaching fellow, the highly gifted Ryan Helfenbein, was a great help to me.

I am deeply indebted to Scott Lamb, a man of great heart and mind who served faithfully for many years as my director of research, and to a cohort of faithful interns, whose energies were a tremendous gift. Those interns who made a special contribution to this book include Mat Alexander, Chris Parrish, Matt Tyler, and Ryan Hoselton. They were always ready to run for an article or track down a source. My librarian, Drew Griffin, was tremendously helpful, as always.

Robert and Andrew Wolgemuth at Wolgemuth and Associates nourished this project along, and their author representation skills freed me to write the book rather than worry about the details. The team at Bethany House has been most helpful, but special appreciation goes to my editor, Andy McGuire.

Finally, I must acknowledge the vast list of those leaders who have greatly influenced me, starting with my parents and pastors and teachers and extending to some of the most illustrious public leaders of our time. Add to these those of the past, on whose shoulders we still stand.

Leaders are made by other leaders, and are made better by other leaders, and go on to make yet more leaders.

The line of acknowledgment and gratitude never ends, but this list must. In all things, thanks be to God.

R. Albert Mohler Jr.
Louisville, Kentucky

The Conviction to Lead

True Leadership Starts With a Purpose, Not a Plan

Let me warn you right up front—my goal is to change the way you think about leadership. I do not aim merely to add one more voice to the conversation; I want to fundamentally change the way leadership is understood and practiced.

For the better part of the last three decades, leadership has been a major cultural preoccupation and a professional obsession. Walk into an airport bookstore, and you will find the front tables filled with books promising to make you a better leader. Apparently, frequent travelers have a healthy appetite for such advice. Walk into a Christian bookstore, and you will find ample evidence of the same hunger.

If you are like me, you probably have read a small library of books on leadership, have attended numerous conferences and seminars, and keep up with leadership newsletters and professional journals when you find the time. Hotel conference rooms overflow with people listening to speakers deliver talks on leadership, and colleges and universities have gotten into the business as well, offering majors, degree programs, and even entire schools devoted to leadership studies.

And yet something is missing.

I was born in 1959, right at the center of the golden age of American management. The "managerial revolution" was in full swing, and America's corporate leaders were managers of the first rank. But no one really thought of them as "leaders."

President John F. Kennedy took office in 1961, assembling a cabinet of youthful and technocratic managerial experts, largely drawn from America's leading corporations. Writer David Halberstam would later call these men "the best and the brightest." Lyndon Johnson, Kennedy's vice president, was considerably impressed by Kennedy's collection of managerial expertise. When he gushed about them to former Speaker of the House Sam Rayburn, the Speaker retorted, "Well, Lyndon, you may be right and they may be every bit as bright and intelligent as you say, but I'd feel a whole lot better about them if just one of them had run for sheriff once."

We get his point. Those managers were among the brightest of their generation, but they managed the nation right into the disasters of the 1960s, such as the Bay of Pigs and Vietnam. Evidently, management is not the same thing as leadership.

As a teenager I was already looking for examples of leadership. I read about Winston Churchill, and I recognized that he was no mere manager—he was a leader of world-changing courage. When he spoke, a nation was given the hope and determination to fight a war that simply had to be won—against odds that left even many of his own friends and family convinced that England's future was already lost.

I cut my political teeth working as a high school volunteer in Ronald Reagan's campaign for the Republican presidential nomination in 1976. Early that summer no one had to ask me twice to be part of the line welcoming Governor and Mrs. Reagan into War Memorial Auditorium in Fort Lauderdale for a major speech. I got to shake Reagan's hand and then hear him speak. He did not talk about vague policy goals or speak in political bromides. He spoke with passion about ideas and the possibility of changing the way Washington was run.

I recognized that he was a leader and that his leadership was transformational. I knew he believed what he was saying, and I could see that he persuaded others to believe with him. Reagan did not win the nomination in 1976, but he went on to carry forty-nine states in the 1980 presidential election. By that time, regardless of partisan identification, Americans were learning again to look for a leader.

In college I studied political science before ending up as a religion and philosophy major. If my exposure to political science was any indication, those professors cared very little about leadership. Every class seemed like a statistics assignment.

In seminary I had to take classes that were then called "church administration." Trust me on this—the classes had little to do with the church and a lot to do with administration, but nothing to do with leadership.

I had to create my own leadership studies program. You will probably discover, or you may already know, that the same is true for you. I read historical biographies, observed the national and international scene, and began to read the emerging literature on political and business leadership. I took every opportunity to watch leaders up close, spending time with as many of them as I could.

The Leadership Renaissance

Fast-forward a few years to when I was editor of one of the oldest Christian newspapers in the nation. I received a call inviting me to join a small group of Christian leaders for a meeting on national drug policy at the White House. President George H. W. Bush was launching a major new initiative intended to stem the drug problem. The other leaders and I flew together up to Washington, and on the plane I noted that almost all of the pastors were talking about someone I had never heard of before. A California pastor named John Maxwell was recording sessions in which he was training his own staff in leadership.

Pastors were buying his tapes and passing them around like the old Soviet dissidents used to exchange samizdat—forbidden political literature. Before long, John Maxwell was teaching leadership all over the country, and his books were showing up in airport bookstores.

By the 1990s leaders were flocking to Willow Creek Community Church in suburban Chicago, where pastor Bill Hybels had started his series of huge leadership conferences. I attended one of the earliest. By the end of the decade it was hard to even get a seat in Chicago, and most people would have to settle for a regional site elsewhere. What was going on?

The hunger for leadership had reached every sector of our society, including business, government, education, cultural institutions, and, of course, the church. Christians, along with everyone else, wanted to develop leadership.

It was not always so, although it is hard now to imagine a time when leadership had something of a bad name. The twentieth century was a brutal and murderous laboratory for leadership. All you have to do is think of names like Vladimir Lenin, Adolf Hitler, Benito Mussolini, Josef Stalin, and Mao Zedong. In light of these horrors, many people began to wonder if leaders and leadership were themselves the problem.

Theodor Adorno and his colleagues at the University of Chicago suggested this in their 1950 book, *The Authoritarian Personality*. They seemed to claim that any ambition to lead was based on unhealthy psychological needs and would produce dangerous results.

> Wherever Christian leaders serve, in the church or in the secular world, their leadership should be driven by distinctively Christian conviction.

This mentality took root in the culture of the 1960s, where counterculture groups demanded the abolition of many leadership positions, and the larger society grew increasingly nervous about the nature of leadership. Educators followed suit with classrooms in which the teacher's role was to be just a fellow learner, no longer "the sage on the stage."

Of course it didn't work. It couldn't work. The nation needed leaders. Businesses needed leaders. Even antileadership movements needed leaders. And teachers had better know more than their students.

The church desperately needs leaders as well. Congregations and Christian institutions need effective leaders who are authentically Christian—whose leadership flows out of their Christian commitment. Wherever Christian leaders serve, in the church or in the secular world, their leadership should be driven by distinctively Christian conviction. The last three decades have seen the emergence of a renaissance in leadership, and the deep hunger for leaders has never been more evident than now. Like me, you want to grow as a leader in order to be ready for all the leadership opportunities you may be called to accept. So what is the problem? It is not a lack of interest, a shortage of books and seminars, or a dearth of leadership development programs. Nor is the problem a lack of attention to what leaders do and how they do it. The problem is a lack of attention to what leaders *believe* and why this is central.

The Two Cultures of Modern Christian Leadership

The problem is that the evangelical Christian world is increasingly divided between groups we might call the Believers and the Leaders.

The Believers are driven by deep and passionate beliefs. They are heavily invested in knowledge, and they are passionate about truth. They devote themselves to learning truth, teaching truth, and defending truth. They define themselves in terms of what they believe, and they are ready to give their lives for these beliefs.

The problem is, many of them are not ready to lead. They have never thought much about leadership and are afraid that thinking too much about it will turn them into mere pragmatists, which they know they shouldn't be. They know a great deal and believe a great deal, but they lack the basic equipment for leadership. As one proverbial deacon said of his pastor, "Oh, he knows a lot, but he can't lead a decent two-car funeral procession."

The Leaders, on the other hand, are passionate about leadership. They are tired of seeing organizations and movements die or decline, and they want to change things for the better. They look around and see dead and declining churches and lukewarm organizations. They are thrilled by the experience of leading and are ardent students of leadership wherever they can find it. They talk leadership wherever they go and are masters of motivation, vision, strategy, and execution.

The problem is, many of them are not sure what they believe or why it matters. They are masters of change and organizational transformation, but they lack a center of gravity in truth. They often ride one program after another until they run out of steam. Then they wonder, *What now?*

You deserve to know exactly who I am and why I am writing this book. I want to turn the Believers into Leaders and the Leaders into Believers. My goal is to knock the blocks out from under the current models of leadership and forge a new way. I stake my life on the priority of right beliefs and convictions, and at the same time I want to lead so that those very beliefs are perpetuated in others. If our leaders are not passionately driven by the right beliefs, we are headed for disaster. At the same time, if believers cannot lead, we are headed nowhere.

> **Many leaders are masters of change and organizational transformation, but they lack a center of gravity in truth.**

My goal is to redefine Christian leadership so that it is inseparable from passionately held beliefs, and to motivate those who are deeply committed to truth to be ready for leadership.

I want to see a generation arise that is simultaneously leading with conviction and driven by the conviction to lead. The generation that accomplishes this will set the world on fire.

I want to see that happen, and I think you do too.

Leading Is Believing

The Leader Is Driven by Beliefs That Lead to Action

When a leader walks into the room, a passion for truth had better enter with him. Authentic leadership does not emerge out of a vacuum. The leadership that matters most is convictional—*deeply* convictional. This quality of leadership springs from those foundational beliefs that shape who we are and establish our beliefs about everything else. Convictions are not merely beliefs we hold; they are those beliefs that *hold us* in their grip. We would not know who we are but for these bedrock beliefs, and without them we would not know how to lead.

In 1993, I walked into my office as president of the Southern Baptist Theological Seminary for the first time and closed the door behind me. In the months between my election and taking office, I had ample time to understand my challenge. I was called to turn one of the largest and most venerable Christian institutions upside down, taking it back to its founding commitments and convictions. Almost the entire faculty was against me, and they had far more teaching experience and academic tenure than I would ever know. Students were already organized in protest, and a gaggle of reporters was almost permanently staked outside my office.

Just four years earlier, I had graduated with my PhD from that very institution, my own alma mater. Now I was back as president, charged to make changes that my former teachers would fight in every way they knew how.

As that door closed behind me and I drew a quick breath, it was clear that I lacked almost everything any sane search committee should have been looking for in a president of an institution of this historic stature. But I knew one thing—I was driven by the convictions the school used to stand on, the truths that had brought the school into being. These convictions were right, true, and of primary importance. And, just as importantly, I knew I had the conviction to lead.

This is true of all leaders in some sense, but the Christian leader knows this truth in an especially powerful way because conviction is so essential to our Christian faith and discipleship. Our Christian experience begins with belief. That most familiar of all New Testament verses, John 3:16, tells us that God sent Jesus Christ, his only son, "that whoever *believes* in him should not perish but have eternal life" (emphasis added). When Paul and Silas tell their terrified jailer how he can be saved, they express it with powerful and unmistakable simplicity: "*Believe* in the Lord Jesus, and you will be saved, you and your household" (Acts 16:31, emphasis added).

The command to believe is central to the Bible. Christianity is founded upon certain nonnegotiable truths, and these truths, once known, are translated into beliefs. The beliefs that anchor our faith are those to which we are most passionately and personally committed, and these are our convictions. We do not believe in belief any more than we have faith in faith. We believe the gospel, and we have faith in Christ. Our beliefs have substance and our faith has an object.

Put simply, a conviction is a belief of which we are thoroughly convinced. I don't mean that we are merely persuaded that something is true, but rather that we are convinced this truth is essential and life-changing. We live out of this truth and are willing to die for it.

The Bible underlines the fact that conviction is absolutely central to the faithful Christian life. When the author of the book of Hebrews sets out to define and demonstrate what authentic faith looks like, he writes, "Now faith is the assurance of things hoped for, the conviction of things not seen" (11:1). Faith is the full assurance of the facts of what God has done for us in Christ, but its roots lie even before that. As the writer of Hebrews tells us, "By faith we understand that the universe was created by the word of God, so that what is seen was not made out of things that are visible" (11:3). Just a few verses later, he writes that "without faith it is impossible to please him, for whoever would draw near to God must believe that he exists and that he rewards those who seek him" (11:6).

In other words, there are some things we have to believe even before we believe that God saves sinners. First of all, we must be convinced that God exists and that he created this world and rules over it. Without these prior beliefs, we would have no understanding of the gospel of Christ.

But we *do* know these things, and these most powerful of all truths take possession of us and begin to rule in our thinking. While this is true of all Christians, the full strength of conviction is what sets the Christian leader apart. These convictions are the very essence of Christian leadership, and it has always been this way.

Consider Peter and John, the two apostles who, just days after the death and resurrection of Christ, had the courage to stare down the Sanhedrin and defy their order not to preach in public about Jesus. They told the arresting authorities that they simply could not stop telling what they had "seen and heard" (Acts 4:20). Those same beliefs are the convictions that do not allow Christian leaders to be silent today, even in the face of threats and opposition.

Conviction explains the courage of Stephen, the first martyr of the early church, who looked straight at those who were about to stone him to death and told them of the gospel of Christ, convinced that God would protect him, even in death. The apostle Paul was willing to experience beatings, imprisonment, shipwreck, and eventual martyrdom all because of the fact that he was convinced God would keep his promises.

Justin Martyr, one of the leaders of the early church, also serves as a portrait of convictional leadership. Leading members of his own congregation to their mutual execution at the hands of the Roman authorities,

Justin encouraged his people with these words, written to the Roman emperor Antoninus Pius: "You can kill us, but you cannot harm us."

That is authentic leadership in its clearest form—the willingness of people to die for their beliefs, knowing that Christ will vindicate them and give them the gift of eternal life. Thankfully, most of us will never have to experience that kind of leadership challenge. Nevertheless, the convictions remain the same, and so does the function of those commitments in the life and thinking of the leader. We know these things to be so true that we are willing to live for them, lead for them, and, if necessary, die for them.

> At the center of the true leader's heart and mind you will find convictions that drive and determine everything else.

The leadership that really matters is all about conviction. The leader is rightly concerned with everything from strategy and vision to team-building, motivation, and delegation, but at the center of the true leader's heart and mind you will find convictions that drive and determine everything else.

Many of my most encouraging and informative models of convictional leadership come from history. Throughout my life I have drawn inspiration from the example of Martin Luther, the great Christian Reformer of the sixteenth century, who was so convinced of the authority of the Bible that he was willing to stand before the intimidating court of religious authorities that had put him on trial, and even to stare down the Holy Roman emperor and declare, "Here I stand. I cannot do otherwise. God help me."

Here I stand. These words are a manifesto of convictional leadership. But Luther was not merely ready to stand; he was ready to lead the church in a process of courageous reformation.

I was a teenager the first time I saw the movie *A Man for All Seasons*, based on the play by Robert Bolt. At the center of the story stands Sir Thomas More, who is eventually on trial for his life. King Henry VIII is furious that More, who had been the lord chancellor of the realm and one of Henry's closest colleagues, would not sign the oath of supremacy that would declare the king to be superior to the church. I later learned that More had himself persecuted the Lutherans and William Tyndale, the great translator of the Bible into English. Bolt's version of Thomas More did not tell the whole truth, but from the first time I saw that film until now, I have been inspired by the example More set as he went to the scaffold in order to be true to his convictions. Facing the crowd gathered to witness his execution, Sir Thomas More stated, "I am commanded by the king to be brief, and since I am the king's obedient servant, brief I will be. I die His Majesty's good servant, but God's first."

That is the kind of conviction that makes all the difference. Sadly, far too many of today's leaders seem to have little idea of what they believe, or are driven by no clear and discernible convictions. How many of today's leaders are known for being willing to die—or even to live—for their convictions?

You can divide all leaders into those who merely hold an office or position and those who hold great convictions. Life is too short to give much attention to leaders who stand for little or nothing, leaders who are looking for the next program or riding the latest leadership fad, trying on idea after idea but driven by no deep convictions.

I want to be a leader who matters, making a difference with my leadership precisely because my convictions matter. Even in the larger world of politics and world history, we can see the difference between leaders of conviction and leaders who are looking for a safe place to land. Conviction explains how Aleksandr Solzhenitsyn could defy the Soviet regime, writing books that revealed the inhumanity of that repressive government. Conviction explains how President Ronald Reagan could stand in Berlin and, against virtually all political advice, demand, "Mr. Gorbachev, tear down this wall!" Conviction explains how former British prime minister Margaret Thatcher could reject calls for political compromise by responding, "The lady's not for turning." Conviction explains the courage of Martin Luther King Jr. writing his now famous "Letter From Birmingham Jail," and Nelson Mandela giving hope to his people as he was imprisoned on Robben Island.

If you think about it, just about every leader who is now remembered for making a positive difference in history was a leader with strong convictions about life, liberty, truth, freedom, and human dignity. In the long run, this is the only leadership that matters. Convictional leaders propel action precisely because they are driven by deep convictions, and their passion for these convictions is transferred to followers who join in concerted action to do what they know to be right. And they know what is right because they know what is true.

How could any Christian leader be satisfied with anything less than this? Positions and offices and titles fade faster than ink. I recently took my son, Christopher, on a trip to New York City. Several times we found ourselves looking at statues and monuments to men who were, at some point, famous or powerful. Most have faded from all memory, their likenesses now blending in with the New York landscape, millions passing by without even giving them a second's notice.

> Without conviction, nothing really matters, and nothing of significance is passed on.

Think about this: Most Americans consider the president of the United States to be the highest office of secular leadership imaginable. But how many Americans can name even twenty or thirty of the forty-four men who have held that office? When was the last time you heard someone mention Chester A. Arthur or William Henry Harrison? We do remember those who were known for their convictions and for the courage that those convictions produced. This same principle can be extended to every office and position of leadership imaginable. Without conviction, nothing really matters, and nothing of significance is passed on.

I believe that leadership is all about putting the right beliefs into action, and knowing, on the basis of convictions, what those right beliefs and actions are. This book is written with the concern that far too much of what passes for leadership today is mere management. Without convictions you might be able to manage, but you cannot really lead.

For Christian leaders, this focus on conviction is of even greater importance. We cannot lead in a way that is faithful to Christ and effective for Christ's people if we are not deeply invested in Christian truth. We cannot faithfully lead if we do not first faithfully believe.

At the same time, many Christians feel called to lead and are passionately committed to all the right truths, but they are simply not sure where to go from here. In the following chapters we will deal with the practical elements and skills of leadership, which are important issues in their own right. But the starting point for Christian leadership is not the leader but the eternal truths that God has revealed to us—the truths that allow the world to make sense, frame our understandings, and propel us to action.

Writing to the Thessalonians, the apostle Paul encouraged them to know that the gospel had come to them, "not only in word, but also in power and in the Holy Spirit and with full conviction" (1 Thessalonians 1:5). As a Christian leader, I hope and pray that is true of me and of you also. I want to lead "with full conviction." This is the heart of convictional leadership, and it starts with the leader's convictional intelligence.

Convictional Intelligence

The Leader Develops the Capacity to Think in Convictional Terms and Leads Followers to Do the Same

Start talking about intelligence and you are likely to incite a controversy. Do you know your own IQ? If you did, would it reveal your capacity to lead? These may sound like abstract questions, but they matter.

The issue of intelligence is controversial because it is inseparable from all kinds of other issues. Back in the middle of the last century, educators and political leaders thought that the measurement of IQ (intelligence quotient) would be the great key to unlocking the secrets of who would succeed and who would not.

It didn't work. For one thing, the idea of intelligence as mere intellectual ability and knowledge turned out to be fairly unhelpful. To state the obvious, there are plenty of very intelligent people who do not get very far in life. Taking the point one step further, there are plenty of very intelligent people who have virtually no ability to lead.

This is where the theory of multiple intelligences becomes helpful. Some years ago, people began rethinking the way we understand intelligence, especially as it relates to leaders. An educational psychologist at Harvard named Howard Gardner helped to popularize the idea of multiple intelligences. Once you think about the idea, it makes perfect sense. There is not merely one form of intelligence; there are several. Gardner rejected what he called the "one-dimensional view of how to assess people's minds."

Intelligence does start with intellectual capacity and the ability to receive, understand, and use knowledge. But other forms of intelligence are just as necessary. Gardner identified several of these abilities and called them intelligences. He described capacities such as musical intelligence, spatial intelligence, logical intelligence, and linguistic intelligence.

> Financial intelligence will wreck itself without moral intelligence and the guidance of ethical reasoning.

You can probably already see how this would be helpful. If the only thing that mattered to your success was what you knew and your ability to assimilate and use that knowledge, then the intellectuals would be the leaders, the actors, the business tycoons, and the athletes. Needless to say, it doesn't usually turn out that way.

In more recent years, this discussion has led to a discussion about emotional intelligence (EQ) and its ability to predict social success. Daniel Goleman of Rutgers University studied almost two hundred corporations and their leaders. His findings, first published in the *Harvard Business Review*, were shocking:

> When I analyzed all this data, I found dramatic results. To be sure, intellect was a driver of outstanding performance. Cognitive skills such as big-picture thinking and long-term vision were particularly important. But when I calculated the ratio of technical skills, IQ, and emotional intelligence as ingredients of outstanding performance, emotional intelligence proved to be twice as important as the others for jobs at all levels.

As it turns out, the ability to lead people depends on the leader's capacity to develop and deploy what Goleman identified as self-awareness, self-regulation, motivation, empathy, and social skill. That makes a great deal of sense, doesn't it? If the leader lacks these elements of emotional intelligence, it really might not matter how otherwise intelligent he is. Albert Einstein was a genius, but not a leader. Many of the world's most intelligent people lack the emotional and empathetic skills necessary for effective leadership.

Recently, moral catastrophes and scandals on Wall Street and elsewhere in the worlds of business and government have produced calls for the development of moral or ethical intelligence in leaders. Business schools have been rushing to add courses on ethical business behaviors and practices. The reason is simple—financial intelligence will wreck itself without moral intelligence and the guidance of ethical reasoning.

Now, in terms of Christian leadership, all of these insights from the concept of multiple intelligences are helpful, but Christian leaders must develop and operate out of an additional intelligence—*convictional intelligence*. Leaders without emotional intelligence cannot lead effectively because they cannot connect with the people they are trying to lead. Leaders lacking ethical intelligence will lead their people into a catastrophe. But leaders without convictional intelligence will fail to lead faithfully, and that is a disaster for Christian leaders.

Convictional Intelligence Begins With Knowledge

Convictional intelligence is not an innate capacity; therefore, unlike other forms of intelligence, rather than being born with it, you have to develop it. Convictional intelligence is the product of learning the Christian faith, diving deeply into biblical truth, and discovering how to think like a Christian.

Once again, at one level this is the responsibility of every Christian, but it is especially vital for the Christian leader. The Christian faith is heavily invested in knowledge, and specifically the knowledge that is revealed in the Bible. This is why Christians have been at the forefront of education from the very beginning. The church first developed schools for the training of new believers, teaching them the fundamentals of the faith. The church borrowed models from Judaism and classical culture, with the goal of passing Christian knowledge from generation to generation.

In the Middle Ages, the church preserved knowledge in monasteries and abbeys, where monks spent their entire lives copying and preserving texts and teaching. Eventually the church gave birth to the university, which gained its very name from the Christian conviction that all true knowledge comes from God.

But knowledge alone is not everything. When the apostle Paul speaks of the superiority of love over all other good things, he informs us that knowledge will pass away (1 Corinthians 13:8). Knowledge must be accompanied by other commitments and capacities.

Nevertheless, knowledge is fundamental. As a matter of fact, God once spoke of his people being "destroyed for lack of knowledge" (Hosea 4:6). That is a stern warning that should get the attention of every Christian leader.

Contrast the priority of convictional intelligence with the models of leadership that are often found and even admired in some Christian circles. Charisma is a great gift, but it cannot substitute for conviction. The same is true of personality skills, gifts of communication, media presence, and organizational ability. None of these things can qualify a Christian leader when conviction is absent or weak.

Without apology, the Christian leader is a devoted student and a lifelong learner. Convictional intelligence emerges when the leader increases in knowledge and in strength of belief. It deepens over time, with the seasoning and maturing of knowledge that grows out of faithful learning, Christian thinking, and biblical reasoning.

Convictional Intelligence Is More than Knowledge

Knowledge is fundamental, but convictional intelligence is not merely knowledge. If this were the case, all the leader would need is a comprehensive theological and biblical encyclopedia close at hand. This raises the issue of how leaders actually lead: They make decisions and chart a direction.

We humans are complex creatures. God made us in his image, creating within us the capacity to know him and to possess incredible knowledge. He also gave us the ability to process that knowledge and exercise reason. He even gave us the ability to think about thinking. But as the leader exercises the role of leadership, that thinking must be translated into something more automatic, something that does not require a constant process of thinking and rethinking everything the leader knows.

If that sounds complicated, just consider how you awoke, got dressed, and started your morning. By now most of the actions you took have been forgotten. You may not actually remember brushing your teeth, but you did. You did not have to look for the kitchen, because you do not have to think about how to get there. Some mornings you might not remember much about your drive to the office. Why? Your intelligence was at work in all of those actions, but you were primarily operating out of habit, reflex, and intuition—three realities that point to the need for convictional intelligence.

We really are creatures of habit. While this may often seem amusing, it is in fact one of the most necessary coping mechanisms we have. If we had to rethink how to tie our shoes every morning, we would never get anything else done. Much of our lives is lived out of habits of action, and most of these habits never even rise to our active consciousness.

We all know that we have habits of action, but we also operate out of habits of mind. We dig intellectual ruts that our minds grow accustomed to following. We see a face on the television news and put that person in the mental category we assigned her long ago. We think we already know what this person is going to say. We look at the covers of books on the front tables in the bookstore, and we recognize an author. We pause to look more closely at a book by an author we have the habit of liking, and we pass quickly over an author that we have the habit of ignoring.

Our habits of action may not say much about us, but our habits of mind do. It really does not matter if you tie your left shoe first or your right. It does matter, however, if your mental habit is to ignore the significance of the people who surround you.

These mental habits start early. Even as children we are learning how to operate out of habits of thought that, by now, we no longer even think about. The importance of convictional intelligence in the life of the leader comes down to the fact that our intellectual habits must be aligned with Christian truth and knowledge. Otherwise, we say that we believe one thing but operate out of mental habits that run in a very different direction. The Christian leader stands out as one who has developed intellectual habits that are consistent with biblical truth.

We also operate out of intellectual reflexes. When certain things happen, our minds respond by shifting into automatic judgment. This, like habit, is necessary, allowing us to operate in our daily lives. Linguists point out that we develop intellectual reflexes that are assigned even to single words. When you hear the word *murder*, you do not have to ask yourself consciously if this is a good thing or a bad thing. When you hear the word *generous*, you immediately draw a positive judgment. You could not get through a day, or even a single conversation, if you did not possess mental reflexes.

The Christian leader must have mental reflexes that correspond to biblical truth. When something happens or an issue arises, the leader's mind must activate the right intellectual reflex. Once that reflex is engaged, the process of thought is already far down the road. If the reflex is wrong, the leader is in danger—and so are all those he leads.

Some of you might be tempted to think that reflexive decision making is inherently dangerous, and it certainly can be dangerous. The danger lies in developing the wrong leadership reflexes and failing to see the error. Nevertheless, no leader can operate for long without a leadership reflex. The modern leader simply faces too many decisions that demand to be made in short order. Without the right reflexes, the leader will surely be overwhelmed.

Lastly, we all operate out of what can only be called intuition. Some of the decisions we make are explainable only by the fact that something greater than a mere recognition of facts is at work. We do not need intuition to know that $2 + 2 = 4$, but we do need intuition to discern what to do in situations that are not so cut and dried.

A few years ago, my family and I were standing on a train platform in southern France. We were headed for Paris and mainly preoccupied with getting on the right train—no small challenge in some French train stations. As we were standing there, a woman with a young boy of about twelve years old came up to us. Between our horrid French and her broken English we were somehow able to communicate. Her son was headed to Paris on the train without her, and she wanted someone to look out for him until he was safely delivered to his aunt at the Paris terminal. She walked up to me and asked for my help. Of course, we were glad to add the boy to our family as we made our way to Paris.

> Our intellectual habits must be aligned with Christian truth and knowledge.

Think about this for a minute. Why did she pass by so many others on that train platform before choosing us, a family that was from another country? To me the reason was clear. She saw that I was with my wife and two young teenage children. We were, as a matter of fact, laughing about nearly missing the train in Munich. Her eyes told her that she was looking at a family, and family meant safety and dependability. She acted on intuition, because she really had no other choice.

As a leader, you will often know why one alternative is right and another is wrong. Sometimes you will have full intellectual justification for making the decision you know is right and will be able to explain that justification to others. But other decisions and judgments are not so easily explained or understood. Particularly if your decisions are about people, you will often have to become less rational and more intuitional. Sometimes you just have to do what you know is right, even when you are not certain that any intellectual argument fits. This is where intuition comes into play, and the leader will have to lean into intuition every single day.

Insiders at Apple have described Steve Jobs as a master of intuition in matters of style and aesthetics. They tell of him holding the prototype of the iPhone in his hands, closing his eyes, and running his fingers over each surface and angle, ordering modifications until it felt just right to his touch. He just knew how it was supposed to feel.

The Christian leader must develop the right intuitions about matters of far greater importance, for you hold something much more important than an iPhone in your hands and in your trust.

So How Does Convictional Intelligence Happen?

There is no secret here, no special decoder ring, no hidden door. Convictional intelligence comes by what we rightly call the ordinary means of grace. God wants his people to possess convictional intelligence and the fullness of the Christian life, and these come by hearing the Word of God preached, celebrating the ordinances of baptism and the Lord's Supper, and living in the fellowship of believers in a faithful local church.

This is extended through the leader's personal devotional life, prayer, Bible reading, and reading of other Christian books and materials. But while the private acts of devotion are truly important, Christians are not called to grow into faithfulness alone. The Christian life is to be lived within the fellowship and accountability of a local congregation, where the Word is rightly preached and believers mature together. In that context convictional intelligence emerges naturally, along with those Christian intellectual habits, reflexes, and intuitions we desperately need.

Just remember this—the Christian leader who cuts himself off from the ordinary means of grace cannot expect to possess convictional intelligence. Going it alone is a recipe for disaster.

Leadership Is Narrative

The Leader Draws Followers Into a Story That Frames All of Life

I first learned of God's love for me through stories. My parents taught me the stories of the Bible, and I grew up in the golden age of flannel-graph and full-color Sunday school art. I knew the stories of Daniel in the lions' den and David killing Goliath, of Joshua and the battle of Jericho and Moses leading the exodus, of Samson and his strength and Esther and her courage. I could tell you about Zacchaeus and Peter and Lydia and Jonah—all before I could add or subtract.

The most important truths come alive through stories, and faithful leadership is inseparable from the power and stewardship of story. The excellent leader knows how to lead out of the power of the narrative that frames the identity and mission of the people he will lead, and the leader knows how to put his own story into service for the sake of the larger story.

We are narrative creatures, and God made us this way. We are set apart from the rest of the animals, in part because we are the keepers of stories. We cannot even tell each other who we are without telling a story, nor should we try.

Experts on leadership often stress the importance of organizational mission and vision, but these vital realities mean little apart from the story that explains why what we are doing is important in the first place. We need to start with the story and let the rest follow.

So how does that work? Literary critics often point out that trouble lies at the heart of a good story. Something needs to happen—some problem needs to be solved, someone needs rescue, a battle must be fought. The story has power because it tells us how the trouble was resolved, how the child was saved, how the battle was won. We read books and watch movies largely in order to lose ourselves in someone else's story.

The movie *The King's Speech* became a blockbuster for this very reason. A film about a relatively bland British monarch does not sound like much of a thriller, but add the story of his unexpected rise to the throne, his lifelong battle against stuttering, and the needs of the nation as the Third Reich loomed on the horizon, and you have the makings of a great story. It just gets better when the man who helps the king learn to speak is an Australian quack and failed actor.

No organization that exists simply for itself is worth leading. Leaders want to lead organizations and movements that make a difference—that fill a need and solve real problems. That story frames the mission and identity of the organization, and explains why you give your life to it. The excellent leader is the steward-in-chief of that story, and the leader's chief responsibilities flow from this stewardship. Leadership comes down to protecting the story, bringing others into the story, and keeping the organization accountable to the story. The leader tells the story over and over again, refining it, updating it, and driving it home.

I am a history buff. My family has listened indulgently as I have gushed with narration as we have traveled around the nation and much of the world. I can't help talking about the meaning of Pompeii, the liberation of Paris, the Great Fire of London, the division and reunification of Berlin, the Battle of Waterloo. Why? Because we cannot understand the world as it is today without knowing these stories.

We cannot understand what it means to be Americans apart from the revolution that gave the nation its birth, the westward expansion, the Louisiana Purchase, the Civil War, the Gilded Age, and the massive national transformations of the twentieth century. We need to learn about George Washington and Abraham Lincoln, Lewis and Clark, Clara Barton and Frederick Douglass, Theodore Roosevelt and Martin Luther King Jr. Our most effective national leaders have known how to identify with these stories and lead others to do the same, to rally the nation to a cause by making the story central.

This is exactly what Winston Churchill did for the British people in the moment of their greatest peril. He told them over and over again that they were part of a great national drama, participants in a story that was already centuries old—a story of honor and duty, of sacrifice and freedom. In Germany a very different man was telling a very different story. Adolf Hitler was telling the German people a story of Teutonic conquest, racial superiority, and blitzkrieg. Churchill's story was true, while Hitler's story was false, and the future of the human race depended on the right story prevailing.

> **Leadership that matters grows out of the leader's own belief that the story is true, that it matters, and that it must both expand and continue.**

Most leaders do not face a challenge quite like that faced by Churchill, but the lesson remains the same. Leadership that matters grows out of the leader's own belief that the story is true, that it matters, and that it must both expand and continue. The story must be believed with conviction, told with conviction, and stewarded with conviction.

The leader's entire life, in one sense, becomes an extension of this story. The organization or movement is led as the story takes life and is infused with energy. If the story is not worthy of your own life and the lives of others, leave and find a cause worthy of your service. If it is, the leader must recognize that the story is central.

Of course, every individual has his or her own story. The credibility of leadership is based, without question, on the leader's identification of his own story within the organization's story. The leader must articulate how he came to be a part of this story, how it came to possess him, and why he now gives himself to it.

When I visit Texas, I am often impressed with the way Texans make themselves a part of the state's story. Newcomers to the state often say, almost apologetically, "Well, I wasn't born in Texas, but I got here as fast as I could." Seriously?

That is actually a great statement for leaders. If you were born into the story, tell that story over and over again. If not, make clear that you got there as fast as you could—that you are so captivated by this story that you dropped everything to come be a part of it. Your own personal identification with the story is vital and you cannot delegate it. Lean into it and learn to tell it well, but tell it with authenticity.

So is the story of your organization everything? This is where the Christian leader's worldview sets him apart from all others. We are not only the stewards of stories; we are the stewards of *the* story.

The Christian Story as the Story of the Word

The Bible is not just a book of stories. It reveals one grand narrative from beginning to end. Borrowing from literary scholars, many Christians now speak of the Bible's metanarrative—its all-encompassing story line. In the Bible, God has revealed the story that underlies every true story, and in which every other true story finds its meaning.

That is the story of God's determination to glorify himself by saving sinners through the atonement accomplished by his own Son. As Christ himself made clear, every word of Scripture serves to tell this story.

In its irreducible form, this story contains at least four major chapters or movements. In the first, *Creation*, God creates the cosmos and everything within it out of nothing. He creates everything that exists by the power of his Word, and he finds it greatly pleasing. He creates all forms of life, and creates human beings uniquely in his own image, granting us the ability to know him. To Adam and Eve he assigns responsibility to rule over, enjoy, and steward creation, and to multiply.

In the second movement, *The Fall*, Adam and Eve defy God, disobey his command, and suffer the inevitable consequences of God's judgment on their sin. They retain God's image, but it is corrupted by sin. They are cast out of the garden and must work by the sweat of their brows. They will now know death and every physical infirmity that comes with mortality. All of nature shares in the suffering, and nature now knows fury, decay, and trouble. Every single human being is born into a conspiracy of sin from which there is no rescue.

Thankfully, God's plan to save sinful humanity is accomplished in the third movement, *Redemption*. This was promised in the Old Testament, but was fulfilled with the coming of Christ, fully God and fully man, who lived a sinless life and went obediently to suffer death on a cross, dying in our place. God saves us by accepting the substitutionary sacrifice of Christ as full payment for the penalty of sin, and he raised Christ from the dead on the third day, announcing to all the vindication and completion of the Son's saving work. Salvation is declared to all who believe on his name and confess him as Savior and Lord.

But this is not the end of the story. In the fourth movement, *Consummation*, God brings everything to a perfect conclusion with the coming of Christ, the resurrection of the dead, the final judgment, the division of all humanity into either heaven or hell, and the inauguration of a New Creation, ruled over by Christ and his redeemed people. Death and sickness are no more, and all things are brought to their proper conclusion by the sovereign power of God. Among Christ's people, every eye is dry as every tear is wiped away.

This is the greatest story ever told. As Christians, we are to find our identity and meaning in this story and in no other story. It is to be the story that frames our thinking, our living, and our leading. This is the story that tells us who we are, how we got here, and where we are going. This story is the truest and most powerful of all stories, the great metanarrative that frames everything we think, decide, and do. It is also what allows us to die, knowing that the story will survive us and that we are still a part of this story even after our death.

Whatever the context of leadership, the Christian leader is accountable to this story. This is who we are, what we believe, and what we hope for others to know as well. The movements, congregations, and organizations we lead are all a part of it. Even when the Christian leader serves a secular organization, the leader knows that its meaning and mission are fully accountable to this story. The Christian leader can give himself to a worthy secular cause precisely because he knows of God's love for this world and for his human creatures. But the Christian leader can never have a perspective that is limited to this world, no matter how urgent the mission may be.

The conviction to lead is rooted in this story, and it is expressed through our own individual stories and the stories of the organizations we lead. The leader is entrusted with the stewardship of these stories, and no leader can lead well if this story is not his own.

> The Christian leader can never have a perspective that is limited to this world, no matter how urgent the mission may be.

The leader also knows that the story is not our possession. It possesses us. The leader is deeply and inevitably humbled by the story, because it—like the gospel—reminds us that every office or position of leadership comes to us by grace.

The story is so important that we got here as soon as we could. Now there is much good work to be done. There are battles to be fought. There are people to serve and needs to be addressed. There are people to reach and new opportunities to seize. The leader's enthusiasm comes directly from the story and the organization's energies flow along with the story.

This is convictional leadership. The convictional leader does not love and live the story because he knows that it is powerful. He knows that it is powerful precisely because it is true.

Leaders Understand Worldviews

The Leader Shapes the Worldview of Followers

Leadership is the greatest intellectual challenge I can imagine. Let's be honest—leadership would be easier if human beings were less complex, but complex beings we are. Even our thought life is more complicated than we often realize.

Years ago, the economist Thomas Sowell wondered why the same people tend to end up on opposing sides of controversies. The issues are not the same, but the lines of division often are. After observing this pattern for some years, Sowell came to this basic conclusion: People do not think issue by issue and question by question. Instead, they operate out of what he called a vision—a basic understanding of reality.

In Sowell's words, visions are "the silent shapers of our thoughts." These visions shape our thoughts without most people even being aware that it is happening. Leaders need to know this and to recognize that if we are not shaping these "silent shapers," we are failing to lead.

Sowell's point is worth a closer look. In his words:

> Visions may be moral, political, economic, religious, or social. In these and other realms, we sacrifice for our visions, and sometimes, if need be, we face ruin rather than betray them. Where visions conflict irreconcilably, whole societies may be torn apart. Conflicts of interest may dominate the short term, but conflicts of vision dominate history.

He made one additional point that every leader must face squarely: "We will do almost anything for our visions, except think about them."

Well, leaders have to think about them or leadership will never really happen. This is why so many leaders become frustrated or ineffective. They move from one program to the next, from one team to another, doing their best to direct, strategize, and motivate. But at the end of the day, little has changed. Thomas Sowell helps to explain why. The leader never shaped the vision of followers.

How Worldviews Work

When I was in high school, I saw among my classmates what Thomas Sowell observed, and as a Christian I wondered how it all worked. About that time the writings of Francis Schaeffer started to make an impact on young Christians. Schaeffer was something new on the scene, and his lectures and writings caught the attention of a generation of believers tying to figure out the world around them and what difference Christianity was supposed to make.

Schaeffer started talking about the importance of worldviews and the Christian's responsibility to develop a truly Christian mind. He explained that the social and cultural chaos of the 1960s and 1970s was due to collisions between different worldviews—the very thing Sowell would later define as the conflict of visions.

The fundamental idea of a worldview was not Francis Schaeffer's invention, but he did make it accessible to a new generation of evangelical Christians. The word was coined in the German language as *Weltanschauung*, and it quickly migrated into the English language. Once you understand it, your entire approach to leadership will be changed.

Worldviews work by organizing ideas. At the most basic level of our thinking, every single one of us operates out of one unified understanding of the world. As Sowell says, these worldviews are the "silent shapers of our thoughts." You might even say that they are sets of ideas that make the world operational for us. If we did not believe these ideas, we would have no idea how to make sense of the world. We cannot rethink our basic understanding of reality every morning. Basic moral judgments are embedded within our worldview.

Those who believe that our greatest fulfillment must be found in this life will shape their worldview accordingly, and that belief will drive many other beliefs and assumptions. Those who believe that there is no real truth will eventually form a worldview around that assumption. The same pattern holds for all of us. We form a worldview, and then the worldview forms us.

> We cannot rethink our basic understanding of reality every morning. Basic moral judgments are embedded within our worldview.

These basic ideas become the framework for our thoughts, decision making, and way of analyzing issues. Reveal your worldview to me, and I will be able to predict where you stand on any number of issues. If I know what you believe about the nature of human dignity, I can most likely predict where you stand on abortion. Tell me what you believe about moral absolutes, and I can probably guess your position on questions of sexuality and marriage.

A robust and rich model of Christian thinking—the quality of thinking that culminates in a God-centered worldview—requires that we see *all* truth as interconnected. Ultimately, the wholeness of truth can be traced to the fact that God is himself the author of all truth. Christianity's doctrines are not like separate tools in a mechanic's belt to be used only when needed. Instead, Christianity is a comprehensive worldview and way of life that grows out of Christian reflection on the Bible and the unfolding plan of God revealed in the unity of the Scriptures.

A God-centered worldview brings every issue, question, and cultural concern into submission to all that the Bible reveals, and frames all understanding within the ultimate purpose of bringing greater glory to God. This task of bringing every thought captive to Christ requires more than haphazard Christian thinking, and is to be understood as the task of the church and not merely the concern of individual believers. The recovery of the Christian mind and the development of a comprehensive Christian worldview will require the deepest theological reflection, the most consecrated application of scholarship, the most sensitive commitment to compassion, and the courage to face all questions without fear.

Christianity brings the world a distinctive understanding of time, history, and the meaning of life. The Christian worldview contributes an understanding of the universe and all it contains that points us far beyond a material world that came about only through time and chance. Christians understand that all of creation is dignified by the very fact that God has created it. At the same time, we understand that we are to be stewards of this creation and are not to worship what God has made. We understand that every single human being is made in the image of God and that God is the Lord of life at every stage of human development. We honor the sanctity of human life because we worship the Creator. From the Bible, we draw the essential insight that God takes delight in the ethnic and racial diversity of his human creatures, and so must we.

The Christian worldview includes a distinctive understanding of beauty, truth, and goodness, understanding these to be, in the final analysis, one and the same. Thus, the Christian worldview rejects our culture's attempts to separate the beautiful from the true or the good. Christians consider the stewardship of cultural gifts, ranging from music and visual art to drama and architecture, as a matter of spiritual responsibility.

The Christian worldview understands society's need for law and a proper respect for order. Informed by the Bible, Christians understand that God has invested government with an urgent and important responsibility. At the same time, because of the Fall, Christians come to understand that idolatry and self-aggrandizement are the temptations that come to any regime. Drawing from the Bible's rich teachings concerning money, greed, the dignity of labor, and the importance of work, Christians have much to contribute to a proper understanding of economics. Those who operate from an intentionally biblical worldview cannot reduce human beings to mere economic units, but must understand that our economic lives reflect the fact that we are made in God's image and are thus invested with responsibility to be stewards of all the Creator has given us.

Christian faithfulness requires a deep commitment to serious moral reflection on matters of war and peace, justice and equity, and the proper operation of a system of laws. Our intentional effort to develop a Christian worldview requires us to return to first principles again and again in a constant and vigilant effort to ensure that the patterns of our thought are consistent with the Bible and its master narrative.

Every Christian has the responsibility to develop a worldview that is authentically Christian, but leaders face that duty in a way that is even more urgent. We have to be faithful in the discipleship of the mind before we can expect faithfulness and maturity in those we lead.

Leaders as Worldview Shapers

Far too often leaders aim at the surface level and stop there. Real leadership doesn't happen until worldviews are changed and realigned. You might be able to lead a group to build a house without trying to shape worldviews, but you cannot build a movement that way.

Leadership is the consummate human art. It requires nothing less than that leaders shape the way their followers see the world. The leader must shape the way followers think about what is *real*, what is *true*, what is *right*, and what is *important*. Christians know that all truth is unified, and so these concerns are unified as well. Leaders aim to achieve lasting change and common alignment on these questions.

As the old saying goes, reality may be a difficult concept, but it is even more difficult to try to live without it. Leaders must work to put every member of the group or movement on the same field of reality. This world is real, but the world to come is even more real. We are real, but our reality is entirely dependent upon God. Christians affirm that reality exists and that it can be known, and we put a premium on knowing what it is, and knowing how to distinguish the real from the unreal. Leaders must be unquestionably committed to the truth, and they must lead their followers to do the same. Beyond that, leaders must lead followers into a growing maturity that enables them to discern the true from the false. Christianity is so deeply invested in truth because Christ declared that he is "the way, the truth, and the life" (John 14:6).

> The effective leader changes the way followers think about the world.

Leaders are directed by the knowledge of what is right, and nothing is so inseparable from leadership as morality. But the leader must not only know what is right, do what is right, and lead in the direction that is right—he must also lead followers to embrace this same knowledge.

Matters of priority are also central to worldviews, and the leader must teach followers what is most important, most urgent, and most essential. If not, followers will go off in different directions, working out of very different understandings of what matters most. The great aim of leadership is to lead followers continually into a deeper and more comprehensive love for what is most real, most true, most right, and most important. The thrill of leadership is in seeing this happen, and long-term success depends on it.

The organization, institution, or congregation you lead will never achieve anything great or worthy unless an alignment of worldview takes place, and the leader bears the responsibility to make that happen. Over time, those who share that worldview most fully will gravitate to the center of the organization's leadership and energy. Those who share the worldview less fully will migrate to the periphery of the organization, and may even exit.

This is how effective, faithful leadership works. You aim at the heart and the head of your followers, confident that if they share the worldview and embrace it with conviction, the right actions will follow naturally.

Richard Weaver had it right when he flatly stated that "ideas have consequences." They do indeed. Ideas drive history, and ideas shape other ideas. That is why the reality of a worldview is so important. The effective leader changes the way followers think about the world. What could be more exhilarating than that?

6

The Passion to Lead

Passionate Leaders Driven by Passionate Beliefs Draw Passionate Followers

"How badly do you want this position?" The question was thrown at me out of the blue, but I knew how to answer it. I said that I thought I had been born for this job and that there was no chance I would not take it if offered. Frankly, I had not expected to be so candid, but once he asked the question, my answer was set.

The man who asked me that question was a consultant hired by the search committee that eventually nominated me to become president of the Southern Baptist Theological Seminary. I had not looked forward to the conversation, having been told that it was to be about psychological factors. Honestly, I am not sure how a psychologist would assess my answer, but it fit what the search committee was looking for—a leader who believed he was the right man for the job.

Leaders need to possess and develop many qualities, but the one element that drives them to the front is passion. Without it, nothing important happens.

Sometimes the absence of passion is easy to spot. No one described this problem better than Søren Kierkegaard, the philosopher sometimes called the "Melancholy Dane." Kierkegaard was a man of the early nineteenth century, and his thought eventually gave rise to what became known as existentialism, a philosophy that focuses on the importance of the individual's experience. In that sense, Kierkegaard might seem an odd person to bring to a conversation about leadership. Nevertheless, he has something really important to say when it comes to passion.

Looking at the churches in Denmark in his day, Kierkegaard decided that their pastors must not believe what they were teaching. After all, they were preaching the most revolutionary and transformative message human ears had ever heard—the gospel. But the church looked lifeless, and its pastors seemed to be going through the motions. The churches had fine stained glass and beautiful music, but Kierkegaard declared that they lacked the one thing most necessary—passion.

Kierkegaard contrasts passion with mere "flashes of enthusiasm." Passion is not a temporary state of mind. It is the constant source of energy for the leader, and the greatest cause of attraction for followers. Finally, Kierkegaard reminds us that passion cannot be artificially generated or transmitted. If authentic, it naturally shines through as convictions come to life, as a great mission is undertaken, and as people share the same great passion and join together as one.

Like so many of life's most important realities, passion is more often sensed than defined. We know it when we see a leader who naturally draws others into the vortex of their leadership.

What Produces Passion?

If passion could be made into a pill, every leader would take it and distribute it to every member of their organization. It doesn't work that way, of course. We cannot buy passion, nor can we simply decide to be passionate. Passion must arise out of conviction. It cannot come any other way.

It has been said that Communism never produced a great work of art. The Soviet Union had extensive museums, but the only masterpieces they held were from ages before the Communist revolution. Communism, it turned out, could not inspire artists to great work. That should have been a sign to the leaders of the Soviet Union, for as history records, the Soviet empire fell victim to a lack of passion. As soon as the empire began to crumble, it became clear that no one seemed determined to save it from collapse.

The issue was not that the Soviet Union lacked power—it was one of the world's two superpowers. The problem was the beliefs that undergirded the Soviet experiment. Those beliefs produced a murderous state with an unwieldy bureaucracy and, in the end, incompetent leaders. Communist convictions had produced these leaders, but even they lacked all passion for Communism in the end.

> **Passion is not a temporary state of mind. It is the constant source of energy for the leader, and the greatest cause of attraction for followers.**

Passion arises naturally or not at all. It happens when convictions come to life, and deep beliefs drive visions and plans. The passionate leader is driven by the knowledge that the right beliefs, aimed at the right opportunity, can lead to earth-shaking changes.

Just look around the business world. The leaders who are most transformative and effective are those who believe most deeply in what they are doing, in the theory of their own business. Steve Jobs really believed that people would be empowered by technology. Henry Ford really thought that the cause of humanity would be greatly advanced by the development of the automobile, the living wage, and the assembly line.

If you are looking for a CEO for an airline, you had better seek someone who loves planes, who dreams of airplanes and routes in his sleep. That same necessary passion applies to every context of leadership. The president of a university had better believe that education can change both lives and nations. An effective general must truly believe that the disciplined use of force can establish peace. The head of a hospital had better wake up every morning with such passion that he can hardly wait to get to work and see people helped and healed.

The same is true in church life, of course, and at a far deeper level. The most faithful and effective pastors are those who are driven by deep and energizing convictions. Their preaching and teaching are fueled by their passionate beliefs and sense of calling. With eternity hanging in the balance, they know what to do. They see every neighborhood as a mission field and every individual as someone who needs to hear the gospel. They cannot wait until Sunday comes and they can enter the pulpit again, ready to set those convictions loose.

In any context of leadership, passion arises out of beliefs. For the Christian leader, those convictions must be drawn from the Bible and must take the shape of the gospel. Our ultimate conviction is that everything we do is dignified and magnified by the fact that we were created for the glory of God. We were made for his glory, and this means that each one of us has a divine purpose.

The Christian leader finds passion in the great truths of the Christian faith, and especially in the gospel of Jesus Christ. No one who has truly experienced the transforming and redeeming power of the gospel can think of life without passion. Leadership arises from this passion and is driven by it. Other leaders may be driven by a passion for cars or technology or empire building, but the Christian leader is driven by the convictions that give all of life its meaning. Everything else flows from this naturally.

When the effective leader sees a problem, the passion to solve it comes from within. The convictions and beliefs are already in place, and they allow the leader to see and define the need or opportunity. Almost like a reflex, the leader finds that plans and strategies and ambitions are coming into view, along with an insatiable motivation to see the right things happen.

This is the essence of passionate leadership, but the passion cannot stop with the leader.

Passion Is Contagious

Passionate leaders attract and motivate passionate followers. Together, they build passionate movements. When this happens, anything is possible.

A few years ago I was asked to preach at a church in the middle of an Ohio cornfield. It was a long way from a major city, but the church had attracted hundreds of members and many visitors. Its pews were filled with young people, and the energy level was incredible. Why were they there? They had been drawn by conviction and motivated by passion. They were bringing their friends to experience what they had come to know in this church.

Over the last several decades, liberal churches and denominations have been losing members by the multiple thousands. It is the conservative churches that are growing—those churches that are most grounded in convictions and most ardent in their beliefs. There is no real mystery why this is so. Once beliefs have been minimized and convictions have been marginalized, energy leaves the movement like air escaping a balloon. The same is true of other arenas of leadership. When the mission is ambiguous and the beliefs of the organization are nebulous, passion dissipates quickly.

On the other hand, leaders with passion transfer that passion to others. Like an infectious disease, passion spreads exponentially through the movement. The leader aims at the maximum rate of contagion, modeling that passion in everything that is said and done. Before long, passion takes hold of the entire movement and lasts for the long haul.

The Language of Passion

Leaders must learn to use what the Latin American writer Mario Vargas Llosa calls "the language of passion." Leaders must use their brains, but they need to speak from the heart. The most powerful leaders know how to speak the language of passion rather than the language of bureaucracy and dispassionate analysis.

What does this sound like? The passionate leader emphasizes morality and purpose. It is not enough that a decision is workable; it must also be right. The leader cannot be satisfied that a product is adequate; it must enhance the lives of those who use it. A plan cannot be justified with the language of apathetic analysis; it must be presented with the language of passion and purpose.

People who are drawn to a great need will be passionate about meeting it. Those who see a great and worthy opportunity will be energized to seize it and sacrifice for it. Organizations driven by passion thrive on the experience of seeing change happen in the service of common convictions.

The leader has to come back to this level again and again, reminding the movement of its convictions and mission and infusing the movement with fresh passion and vision. When push comes to shove in leadership—and it will—the leader resets the equation by going back to the convictions and leaning into passion. As new people come into the movement, they must be trained in the convictions if they are to share the passion. When trouble is confronted, the leader responds consistently with the convictions in order to protect the passion.

> **Organizations driven by passion thrive on the experience of seeing change happen in the service of common convictions.**

The language of passion requires boldness. Leaders learn to speak of causes, not structures; of movements, not mechanics; of people, not statistics; of cherished principles, not mere policies.

Over time, this comes naturally, but it requires the leader to leave some habits of speech and communication behind. Passion requires Technicolor, not earth tones. There is an infinite difference between the words *might* and *must* when it comes to opportunity. Followers are listening for the verbal cues that indicate passion or betray its absence. This is true of everything the leader says, writes, and represents. If the leader's passion is artificial, the movement will know it. When it is authentic, the movement catches it and passes it along like a contagion.

I was elected president of the institution I serve at a crucial moment in its history. It would go one direction or the other. I had been elected to change its direction radically, and that mission would succeed or fail just as radically. The people who elected me were passionate about the change that was needed and were driven by convictions. The churches in the denomination were convictional as well, and they were passionate about recovering their institutions. They were looking for a leader who would share those convictions, give voice to them, and direct the institution in a completely new direction. That required a large dose of passion.

That's why I was asked the question that opened this chapter. Knowing what was at stake, how badly did I want this job? With all my heart. That is to say, with unbridled passion.

7

Leaders Are Thinkers

Leadership Begins When You Learn to Think Like a Leader, and Leadership Is Not Achieved Until Followers Learn to Think as Well

Before anything else, leadership is an intellectual activity. While it is natural to point to action as the essence of leadership, activity is the result of thinking, and in this first stage of leadership the seeds of eventual success or failure are sown. Our actions may never reach the heights of our thinking, but you can be certain that the quality of your actions will never exceed the quality of your thinking.

Careful attention to thinking is what first sets the leader apart. We introduced this idea in the chapter on convictional intelligence, but here we want to take it a step farther. The fact is that most human beings evidently do not like to think. At the very least, most seem quite satisfied never to think in a concerted, critical, and careful way. Such leaders never think strategically, consistently, or critically. They go from thought to thought without reflection, analysis, or questioning their own decisions. They operate at the basic level of thinking, and they think about the things that interest them, but they are not seriously interested in the process and quality of thought.

Like everyone else, leaders operate out of capacities such as instinct, intuition, and habit. But what sets the leader apart is the commitment to bring these very things under the control of active intellect and right patterns of thinking. When an organization is run well, the average person, and perhaps even the average follower within the organization, might assume that the leader has some secret and almost magical sense of direction and purpose—an instinct or inner voice that seems always to guide with accuracy. In truth, this inner voice is the achievement of devoted thinking, not a gift that simply falls into the leader's lap.

Consider some of the most familiar leadership roles. Coaches of professional athletic teams are known for their instincts, but these "hunches" are actually the products of years of learning and thinking about the game. These intuitions come only after massive learning and experience.

The same is true of generals in the annals of military history. Some seemed to have an instinctive sense of the battlefield. As someone long ago explained, these generals seem able to smell an enemy force from miles away. Nevertheless, you can count on the fact that these instincts were as hard earned as their battles were hard won.

The idea of the leader as mystical guru or shaman is unhealthy and unworkable, especially over time. There may be crises and other occasions when the leader has to function as if direction is coming from mere instinct and intuition, but these occasions had better be rare and truly urgent. Otherwise, the organization will begin to depend upon direction from a guru, and followers will not learn to develop the right patterns of thinking.

This is particularly true for Christian leaders. We do not set ourselves up as prophets or oracles. Instead, we lead out of authenticity and the open acknowledgment that we are doing what all leaders must do—face the facts, lean into the truth, apply the right principles, acknowledge the alternatives, and, finally, make the right decision. In other words, the leader leads by conviction.

The Leader Faces the Facts

Christianity is heavily invested in reality. We believe that God created an orderly world that he intended for us to know. We believe that God created us as rational creatures who have the real, but partial, capacity to understand reality. We can be certain that we are to devote ourselves to understanding reality rather than denying it.

Why is reality such a difficult concept for so many people? The answer is simple—we are often dissatisfied with or afraid of reality, and so we are resistant to accepting it.

The leader faces the facts, and this means that the facts must be determined and known. The leader must know the organization as it is, know its needs as they are, and face the world as it actually exists. The conscious denial of reality is a central danger of leadership, and the leader must defend against this temptation. History is filled with generals who refused to admit they had been out-maneuvered, captains who refused to admit they were lost, and CEOs who refused to admit that no one was buying their products.

In order to do this, the leader must demand to know everything critical and essential to the organization, its tasks, its operating status, its finances, its policies, its history, and its opportunities. The leader must be unafraid of data and facts, and he must surround himself with people who know the information he needs and will give it to him.

The leader starts out by affirming the importance of reality and the crucial facts that must be known, and he makes clear that decision making is going to be accountable to those facts. The data will be investigated, analyzed, poked, prodded, and sometimes taken apart and put together again. The leader assumes the responsibility to work until the facts make sense and a clear picture comes into view.

Of course, knowing the facts is not enough, but it is the necessary place to start.

The Leader Leans Into the Truth

The Christian leader is, by definition, committed to living in truth. This is one of the most distinctive and essential elements of Christian leadership, for it is foundational to the Christian life. As mentioned in an earlier chapter, we are to be people of truth because we are disciples of Jesus Christ, who revealed himself to be "the way, the truth, and the life" (John 14:6).

Thus, the leader's disciplined posture is to lean into the truth and to be unafraid of it. He demands that those around him tell him the truth, and he leads by being the truth teller in chief. He does not allow the organization to be tempted by either dishonesty or self-deception, and he models personal honesty.

We are surely safe in assuming that leaning into the truth has never been easy, even as it remains essential. But our own times have made it particularly difficult. The modern carnival of worldviews includes postmodernists who deny the very existence of truth as a reality outside of themselves. This means that some people today actually believe that truth neither exists nor can be known. They believe that when we say that something is true, we are actually just paying a compliment to the statement—we are saying that we like it better than other, equally true, statements. Worse still, some of the more radical postmodernists have declared that claims to truth are the enemy of human freedom.

No one said leadership was going to be easy. Just a few years ago, the comedian Stephen Colbert invented the perfect word to describe how some people look at truth—*truthiness*. Colbert's point is that these people are not really saying that anything is actually true, only that some things are kind of almost getting close to true. We get his point.

Contrast this way of thinking with the clarity of thought offered by Francis Schaeffer, one of the most influential Christian figures of the last fifty years. As I'd mentioned in a previous chapter, Schaeffer was an apologist and defender of Christian truth who had a great love for young people struggling with the issues of the 1960s and 1970s. Many of these young people—struggling Christians and other seekers of truth—made their way to Schaeffer's little community in the Swiss Alps, known as L'Abri. He made a massive impact on my generation, and on me, through his writings and speaking. Schaeffer insisted that Christians must be committed to what he called *true truth*—to the affirmation that truth exists and can be known.

True truth is the perfect antidote to *truthiness*. The Christian leader leans into truth, knowing that the truth always matters and that nothing less than the truth will do.

The Leader Applies the Right Principles

Facts do not exist as solitary particles of truth. As we discussed in the previous chapter, Christians believe that all truth is God's truth and that truth is unitary and consistent. The Christian leader does not stop thinking once the right facts are determined and affirmed. The next step is to analyze and consider what these facts mean and where they lead.

This requires critical thinking and careful analysis. At this stage the leader takes ideas and thoughts apart and puts them back together again, considering what they mean. This is the crucial stage that requires the most careful thinking, and this is the point at which many leaders fail. The captain of the *Titanic* had been advised that icebergs were in the vicinity. He had the facts. What he lacked was judgment. He did not act as the facts demanded.

Human thought is sequential. Our minds move from one observation to another, from one fact to another, from one idea to another. Disciplined thought requires the leader to think clearly about how things connect and how reality is to be analyzed.

The leader's responsibility is to develop the right habits of mind and patterns of thought. Ideas and observations must be tested and the truth must be trusted. False data must be rejected and extraneous information must be put aside. The leader develops a disciplined mind, committed to Christian truth and guided by scriptural principles. The leader is committed to the development of a comprehensive worldview based in truth and to the consistent application of truth to decision making. This is the essence of convictional leadership and the faithful operation of convictional intelligence.

The Leader Acknowledges the Alternatives

If the right decision were always clear to everyone, we would not need leaders. Leaders must know the way the organization should be directed and the course that must be taken, but they also need the skill to motivate others to follow that lead.

Experienced leaders often arrive at this point quite naturally, and are ready to pull the trigger and make a decision. Though understandable, this is dangerous. Leaders must identify the alternatives, and they must do so openly and clearly. The existence of different possible decisions is what makes the leader essential, and leadership does not really happen until the right course is chosen and the organization responds with the right action and corresponding energy. But before the decision is fully made, the alternatives must be acknowledged. Otherwise, the leader may rush past an alternative that did not look so promising when first considered, but is now clearly the best option.

> **Leaders who fear acknowledging alternatives to their decisions undermine their own credibility.**

The leader serves the organization for the long term by constantly articulating the alternatives. Given the situation, we could move in directions A, B, or C. The process of analysis and convictional thinking is what gives the leader the right answer, and the organization needs to understand how and why. The wise leader lays out the alternatives and then walks the organization through the process of understanding which decision or direction is best. The inferior alternatives—the roads not taken—are acknowledged.

A leader's direction and decision making are tremendously enhanced by this stage of leadership. Followers learn that decisions are made with strategic thinking, care, and a commitment to truth, and on the basis of convictional intelligence. Leaders who fear acknowledging alternatives to their decisions undermine their own credibility. Oracles have to be infallible. Leaders only have to be right—and that means getting to the right decision for the right reasons.

Leaders Make the Right Decision

This can be a very dangerous statement, because any leader will make some bad decisions. I can certainly think of no shortage of bad decisions I have made as a leader. As a matter of fact, I have sometimes called in a colleague to complain about a project or program that just doesn't seem to be firing on all cylinders. When I have asked, "Whose idea was this?" more than once I have been told, "That idea was yours." But the leader has to make the right decision most of the time, even almost all the time, or the organization needs a new leader.

The most effective leaders make the right decisions over and over again and develop credibility even as they gain experience. The leader is, as President George W. Bush famously insisted, the decider. The buck stops at the leader's desk, and that is why your name is on the letterhead.

So why is decision making such a challenge for some people? We all know of those in leadership positions who seem to make vacillation a virtue. This is disastrous. Organizations suffer and even die by indecision, but some people seem to have little or no confidence in their decision-making ability. Are they missing a decision-making gene? No, they lack the courage of their convictions, the discipline of critical thinking, or the confidence of steady leadership.

So what's the antidote to these problems? It is following the right pattern and progression of thought. The leader who faces the facts, leans into truth, applies the right principles, and acknowledges the alternatives will then be ready to make the decision—the *right* decision.

Leaders Are Teachers

The Effective Leader Is the Master Teacher Within a Learning Organization

One of the most important questions we can ask someone is, "Who has most influenced your life?" Most of us will quickly point to parents, and then to a teacher. Look at just about any list of influencers named by people in this context, and teachers rise right to the top. Why? The reason is simple. Teachers change the way we see the world, and they often change the way we understand ourselves.

Researchers at Harvard and Columbia universities recently documented in economic terms the difference a great teacher can make. Testing the effectiveness of teachers in the fourth grade, these researchers found that students in a class taught by a great teacher outperformed students in a class taught by a mediocre teacher. This better performance continued all through college and the students' later careers. Just one year made a lasting impact. On average, having a top-notch teacher raised a child's cumulative lifetime income by $50,000.

Right now I can think of several teachers who changed my life. Some of them excited me about new subjects of learning; others encouraged me to push on in my ambitions. A few saw in me what I did not even see in myself. The most powerful of them changed the way I understand the world. These teachers gave me tools for learning that altered the trajectory of my life. They teach me still, years after I sat in their classrooms.

Every great leader is a great teacher, and the greatest leaders seize every opportunity to teach well. Ideas do drive the world, and beliefs determine actions. The leader who wants to effect long-term, lasting, determinative change in an organization has to be its lead teacher, changing minds in order to transform the organization.

The Rise of the Learning Organization

The larger world of corporate leadership and management has discovered the necessity of developing what is now often called a learning organization. The knowledge economy is not a passing fad—it is the shape of the future. Organizations that do not learn will be left behind, and this is true across the spectrum of business and institutional life. The organization of the future will learn fast, learn well, learn together, and learn to keep on learning. The leader who makes the greatest impact will be a master teacher who trains leaders at every level in the organization to teach with faithfulness, enthusiasm, and confidence.

David A. Garvin of the Harvard Business School has defined a learning organization as "an organization skilled at creating, acquiring, and transferring knowledge, and at modifying its behavior to reflect new knowledge and insights."

Though written with the business world in mind, that definition of a learning organization also perfectly fits the mission of the church and the essence of Christian leadership in general. As a matter of fact, it states the mission of any organization that will survive any length of time with its mission and effectiveness intact. We want to change the world by changing the way people think and then deploying them through organizational structures that set them loose in the world to accomplish great things. Leaders are the catalysts for making that happen.

Teaching Is at the Heart of Christianity

The emphasis on the leader as teacher might be a recent arrival in business schools, but it should be second nature to Christian leaders. After all, the Bible elevates teaching to the first mark of the church and the church's primary responsibility. The Great Commission is a command to go and make disciples of the nations, "teaching them to observe all that I have commanded you" (Matthew 28:20).

In this sense, the church was just following in the footsteps of Israel. The Old Testament reveals Israel to be a people whose very survival depended upon teaching. God commanded the fathers of Israel to teach their children according to his Word, and to tell them the story of God's deliverance of his people over and over again. God commanded his people through Moses, stating:

> And these words that I command you today shall be on your heart. You shall teach them diligently to your children, and shall talk of them when you sit in your house, and when you walk by the way, and when you lie down, and when you rise.
>
> Deuteronomy 6:6–7

Every father was to be a teacher, and every teacher was to tell the story over and over again, lest any future generation forget.

> "When your son asks you in time to come, 'What is the meaning of the testimonies and the statutes and the rules that the LORD our God has commanded you?' then you shall say to your son, 'We were Pharaoh's slaves in Egypt. And the Lord brought us out of Egypt with a mighty hand. And the Lord showed signs and wonders, great and grievous, against Egypt and against Pharaoh and all his household, before our eyes. And he brought us out from there, that he might bring us in and give us the land that he swore to give to our fathers.'"
>
> Deuteronomy 6:20–23

This emphasis on teaching explains, to a great degree, why the Jews have survived through so many centuries. By the time of Jesus, the most revered title in Israel was that of rabbi, or teacher. Similarly, the New Testament continues to emphasize the teacher in the life of the church. Leadership is explicitly centered in the responsibility to teach, and the very act of following Christ is defined as discipleship. This, in essence, comes down to teaching one's followers, as Jesus himself modeled.

The command to teach takes on such a role within the church that believers who by now "ought to be teachers" (Hebrews 5:12) are strongly encouraged to mature and take on the teaching role. As in Israel, the church is to be preserved by a succession of faithful teachers. Paul the apostle told Timothy, his protégé, "What you have heard from me in the presence of many witnesses entrust to faithful men who will be able to teach others also" (2 Timothy 2:2).

And yet the New Testament also contains a warning about the stewardship of teaching, and a bracing reminder of why the leader bears a high responsibility. James the apostle wrote, "Not many of you should become teachers, my brothers, for you know that we who teach will be judged with greater strictness" (James 3:1).

This is an important statement. We do not take up the responsibility of leadership without exposing ourselves to the higher standard of God's judgment. In the secular world, leaders worry about the judgment of stockholders and stakeholders. Politicians worry about the verdict of history.

As Christian leaders we know that we will face nothing less than a divine judgment on our leadership.

A Revolutionary Understanding of Teaching

Why do we teach? Why must leaders be so concerned with developing the skills and passions of teaching?

A revolutionary way of understanding the role of the leader as teacher comes from what might be considered an unexpected source—an African bishop from the fifth century. Of course, this is no ordinary bishop, but Augustine, the greatest mind of the early centuries of the church, perhaps the most influential thinker in the church's history. Augustine was born to teach, and, as a teacher of teachers, he devoted himself to thinking deeply about how teachers should approach their responsibility. He was grounded in his knowledge of the love of Christ, and he realized that there is really only one worthy motivation to teach, and that is love.

Love undergirds the entire process of learning, taught Augustine. First, the teacher loves those he will teach. The teacher is not only imparting knowledge but also giving a gift, and the motivation for that gift is not any gain for the teacher but that the student will benefit from the knowledge.

Second, Augustine taught that the teacher must love *what* he teaches. You probably know this from your own experiences as both student and teacher. The best teachers are those who simply can't wait to teach something they truly love.

> **The best teachers are those who simply can't wait to teach something they truly love.**

I have always been an enthusiastic student, but I will admit that some courses and subjects have tested my enthusiasm. One of those was chemistry. At every level, I tried my best to get excited about chemicals, reminding myself of how important knowledge of chemistry is to our understanding of the world. It didn't work.

Nevertheless, my high school chemistry teacher loved his work, and he definitely loved chemistry. I think he went to bed every night dreaming of the next morning's first chemistry lesson. To tell you the truth, I credit his love for chemistry as the only reason I learned anything about chemistry at all. He was so excited about it that I wanted to share at least something of his knowledge.

The best teachers are infectious with their enthusiasm and love of what they are trying to teach. We should not be surprised that just as their enthusiasm for their subject is contagious, so is their call to teach. Most of us who lead and teach do so because our own lives were impacted by those who led and taught us.

The third but most important thing that Augustine reminded Christian leaders was that we teach because we first love Christ, who first loved us. While he was most concerned for those who would lead churches, Augustine's point extends to every arena of leadership. Wherever the Christian leader leads, he must do so out of the love of Christ.

Lastly, Augustine defined the ultimate goal of teaching in a powerful way that should reshape every leader's vision of what we do. The old theologian specified that the goal of teaching is to see every student *instructed, delighted,* and *moved.* Now, just think about that. Augustine was writing about 1,500 years before the modern management revolution, long before the emergence of leadership as a major cultural focus. Centuries before modern leadership had turned to concerns like motivation and the feedback loop, Augustine was telling leaders that our job is not done until three things happen.

Those we lead must be instructed so that they know what they need to know in order to be effective. They cannot be faithful followers and make their contribution to the organization if they lack the necessary knowledge.

Nevertheless, possessing the knowledge is not enough. Leadership happens when followers develop nothing less than delight in knowing the convictions that shape the organization, seeing themselves as a part of the organization's story, and finding themselves in its narrative. They develop their own passions within the organization and its mission, and their delight and excitement becomes contagious to others.

But all this would matter little if the organization was not put into motion. Augustine said that the teacher must aim to *move* his students, much as the leader must move followers to action. Augustine was first concerned with what it meant to move followers in terms of emotion and interest, but he was even more concerned that they live faithful lives. Until conviction is transformed into action, it makes no difference in the world.

Leaders Teach and Teachers Lead

The most effective leaders are unstoppable teachers. They teach by word, example, and sheer force of passion. They transform their corporations, institutions, and congregations into learning organizations. And the people they lead are active learners who add value and passion to the work.

To lead with conviction is to seize the role of the teacher with energy, determination, and even excitement. What could be better than seeing people learn to receive and embrace the right beliefs, seeing those beliefs and truths take hold, and then watching the organization move into action on the basis of those beliefs? Managers can do their work by ordering people to do something, but leaders are never satisfied with people taking orders. Leaders want to see every member of the organization learn what must be done, and why. Leaders are not satisfied until every individual understands the mission, embraces it, and brings others into it.

> Until conviction is transformed into action, it makes no difference in the world.

Real leaders leave behind any idea of teaching as someone else's job, and instead make themselves into leaders who teach and teachers who lead. When the leader is most effective, teaching and leading become one force of energy. When that happens, expect nothing less than transformation.

Leadership Is All About Character

Leaders Are Trusted When Their Lives Are in Alignment With Their Convictions

Every four years Americans put themselves through the ordeal of democracy, choosing candidates and then electing one of them to serve as president of the United States. You can think of it as the world's most public exhibition of the quest for leadership. Election by election, issues and headlines change, but one thing is constant—you can be sure that questions about character will quickly rise to the forefront.

You do not have to be a political scientist to understand why. Americans instinctively know that character matters in leadership. As a matter of fact, you can go so far as to say that character is essential to leadership. People know better than to follow someone they do not trust.

"Character," said President Calvin Coolidge, "is the only secure foundation of the state." Keep in mind that he said that long before the existence of the Internet and instant news. If anything, President Coolidge actually understated the reality. Character is in fact the only secure foundation of leadership itself—any form of leadership.

Leaders are not machines, nor are their followers. We are flesh and blood human beings who have to make constant judgments about trust and confidence. There seems to be an instinct within us to gravitate toward those we can trust and to look warily at those who inspire no such confidence. Within us lies a sort of trust monitor that is constantly running, and we learn to depend on it even as children.

Leadership is as old as humanity, and so is the concern for character in leaders. The Greek and Roman ideals of leadership that were developed in classical antiquity put the emphasis on virtue. The ideal ruler was thought to be the man who embodied the virtues most admired by the people. Some, such as Caesar Augustus and Emperor Marcus Aurelius, were considered almost the incarnation of those virtues. Others, such as Nero and Caligula, were seen to be the very opposite—rulers who rejected those virtues and now bear the severest verdict of history.

America's founding fathers adopted the model of leadership honored by the classical Greeks and Romans. When he was only sixteen, George Washington began the self-conscious attempt to make himself noble and adopted a set of moral maxims by which he intended to live his life. He wanted to be a public man, and he took on classical virtues. When he had won the War of Independence, he retreated to his Virginia estate as a man of peace, following the example of Cincinnatus, the Roman consul who retired from public life after he saved the empire. Of course, Washington was not retired from public life for long.

When the Constitution of the United States was ratified in 1789, the new office of the presidency was actually modeled to fit Washington, and the citizens seemed to recognize that he alone was right to be the nation's first chief executive. In his fascinating study of the founders, historian Gordon Wood explains that Washington, along with John Adams, Thomas Jefferson, and so many others, was not so concerned with the private sphere as he was with public life. He shows that "their idea of character was the outer life, the public person trying to show the world that he was living up to the values and duties that the best of the culture imposed on him." The founders were not unconcerned with private virtue, but they understood that public character was the single most important qualification for public leadership.

For centuries, this model of character in leadership worked well—remarkably well, in fact. But it doesn't work anymore. Scandals, crises, and the burden of history have revealed the cracks in the statues of those who lived and led by public virtue alone. We now look for leaders who are more than a public persona. We look for those whose lives are in full alignment with their convictions.

> **In the world of national politics, Americans have shown that they are not looking for moral perfection, but they are looking for moral stability and conviction.**

Some are unhappy with this. Richard Reeves, biographer of President John F. Kennedy, complains that "the current political debate as it revolves around character issues is literally destroying American politics." I strongly disagree. In the world of national politics, Americans have shown that they are not looking for moral perfection, but they are looking for moral stability and conviction.

Peggy Noonan, speechwriter and biographer of President Ronald Reagan, makes this point:

> In a president, character is everything. A president doesn't have to be brilliant. . . . He doesn't have to be clever; you can hire clever. . . . You can hire pragmatic, and you can buy and bring in policy wonks. But you cannot buy courage and decency; you can't rent a strong moral sense. A president must bring those things with him.

Our difficulty in dealing with the question of character is directly related to the fact that we have no common concept of what character really is. University of Virginia sociologist James Davison Hunter explains that the American people demand character, but the concept of character lacks any public content—we don't have a generally accepted standard by which to measure it. He argues that American culture is so deeply influenced by psychological approaches that moral character has become subjective. Lacking a clear concept of character, most Americans just hope for the best.

As Hunter explains, "Character matters, we believe, because without it, trust, justice, freedom, community, and stability are probably impossible." But if we reduce *character* to a meaningless word used to evoke positive feelings, we aren't likely to find the real thing in those who lead—or in those who follow. Hunter's insight should serve as a lesson in why moral confusion will not work:

> We want character but without unyielding conviction; we want strong morality, but without the emotional burden of guilt or shame; we want virtue but without particular moral justifications that invariably offend; we want good without having to name evil; we want decency without the moral authority to insist upon it; we want moral community without any limitations to personal freedom. In short, we want what we cannot have on the terms that we want it.

Hunter explains the secular confusion well. But this is the point at which the Christian leader has to know a far deeper and urgent call to character—a call to character that is not only a matter of public persona, nor merely a negotiation with the moral confusions of our own age. As followers of Christ, we know that there is no legitimacy to the claim that our private and public lives can be lived on different moral terms. And we also know that the moral terms to which we are accountable are not set by us; they are revealed in God's Word.

"As he thinks in his heart, so is he" (Proverbs 23:7, NKJV). The Bible reveals that character is a condition of our hearts. The Old Testament contains the laws by which Israel was to learn character, and the New Testament presents the church as a community of character. Jesus told his disciples they were to live before the world so that their character would be so apparent that people would give thanks to God.

"You are the light of the world. A city set on a hill cannot be hidden. Nor do people light a lamp and put it under a basket, but on a stand,

and it gives light to all in the house. In the same way, let your light shine before others, so that they may see your good works and give glory to your Father who is in heaven."

Matthew 5:14–16

As a community of character, Christians are to reflect the moral commitments to which we are called. As Jesus made clear, the moral credibility of the gospel depends on those who have been transformed by the grace and mercy of God demonstrating that transformation in every dimension of life. Within the church, leadership falls on those whose light shines with integrity and power.

Duke theologian Stanley Hauerwas rightly points to the fact that, in the eyes of the world, the church's existence as a community of character is what sets it apart. The church is to live by God's Word and the gospel in such a way that others are left scratching their heads, wondering how people could actually live like this. Why do they love each other? Why are they so generous? Why do they stay married to their spouses? Why do they live so conscientiously?

> Within the church, leadership falls on those whose light shines with integrity and power.

The effective leader knows that the expectation of character begins at the top. Those we lead will expect us to live and to lead in alignment with our convictions. They will not be satisfied with character that is lived out only in public, a pretense of our real selves. They are hungry and thirsty for real leadership and real leaders. They have seen where leadership without character leads, and they want no part of it.

Once we state our convictions, we will be expected to live them out in public and in private. The convictions come first, but the character is the product of those convictions. If not, our leadership will crash and burn.

So does alignment with convictions mean that the leader must be perfect? Thankfully, this is not the standard. So what is?

Martin Luther, the great Reformer of the church in the sixteenth century, had a profound awareness of his sin—even after his salvation.

He knew that he was a great sinner in need of a great Savior, and he found salvation and the forgiveness of sin in Jesus Christ. He became a bold, courageous, and brilliant defender of the gospel. He led a reform of the church, transformed Germany, translated the Bible into common German, taught pastors, preached regularly, and was what most of us would now recognize as a workaholic.

But for all of his awareness of the grace and mercy of God in Christ, he was troubled by his own sins. Bold by day, he could also be fearful at night. Prophetic in the pulpit, he could also be short-tempered to his closest friends. Confident without question in the truth of the gospel, he could also feel the tugs of periodic doubt.

> **Character is indispensable to credibility, and credibility is essential to leadership.**

This led Luther to one of his greatest insights into the Christian life. Christians are, he said, simultaneously justified sinners, but sinners still. We are saved, and yet we still struggle with sin. This will not always be the case, for we will one day be glorified. But until then, we still have ourselves to deal with.

This is the leader's responsibility—to deal with himself. We are not perfect, and claims of perfection will only serve to undermine our leadership. We will fail, and we must be answerable for those failures. Our sin will show up in our leadership, usually without delay.

Character is indispensable to credibility, and credibility is essential to leadership. The great warning to every leader is that certain sins and scandals can spell the end of our leadership. We can forfeit our role as leader and the stewardship of leadership can be taken from us.

When our lives are shown to be at odds with our convictions, we destroy everything we have sought to build. At the very least, inconsistency in our lives gives license for others to nurture their own inconsistencies. At its worst, moral and convictional failure spell disaster from which the leader has no way to recover.

Leaders, like all sinners, can be forgiven. But forgiveness does not restore credibility, and character must be seen as something that can be lost far easier than gained, much less restored.

Leaders of character produce organizations of character because character, like conviction, is infectious. Followers are drawn to those whose character attracts them as something they want for themselves. Fairly regularly, we see debates over the meaning of character in leadership and public life. Most of it is nonsense. We know that character matters when we hire a baby-sitter. How can it not matter when we are calling a leader?

Leadership and Credibility

Leadership Happens When Character and Competence Are Combined

No leader can be effective without character, but character does not ensure that a leader is effective. There are many people with sterling character who are not leaders. A good leader stands out when character is matched by competence and the central virtue of knowing what to do.

Most of us think of credibility in moral terms, and with good reason. Credibility defines our ability to trust, and that trust is a matter of character. But leadership requires trust in something beyond who the leader is. True credibility rests in the ability of others to trust what the leader can *do*.

Credibility is not a function of office or title. History reveals many presidents, monarchs, and generals who could not lead. Any number of roads can lead to the corner office, and some of them have nothing to do with leadership. In a massive study of American leadership, James Kouzes and Barry Posner identified credibility as the single most important issue in establishing effective leadership. As they explain:

> Leadership may once have been conferred by rank and privilege. It may once have been something that was characterized by a command-and-control, top-down, do-as-I-say style. But no more. Those days are long gone. Today, leadership is an aspiration. It is something you have to earn every day, because on a daily basis, people choose whether or not they're going to follow you. It's something you keep trying to achieve and never assume you've fully attained.

In my judgment, that is one of the most important passages on leadership written in recent decades. Kouzes and Posner are exactly right when they insist that leadership is "a relationship between those who aspire to lead and those who choose to follow."

> **True credibility rests in the ability of others to trust what the leader can do.**

Once the relational nature of leadership is firmly in mind, leaders understand that their effectiveness requires a faithful transaction—they aspire to lead, and followers receive that aspiration with trust and confidence. Take that trust and confidence away, and the leader is leading no one.

Enter the Leader

When you enter the room, trust and confidence had better enter with you. If not, leadership is not happening. How could it? Leadership is about a sense of direction and purpose, and a competence that puts the room at ease. The leader is not a superman, but he had better know who he is, what he is doing, what the organization faces as a challenge, and how to move forward.

If someone else possesses those fundamental competencies, that person is the leader, not you. If no one in the room possesses those competencies, the organization faces imminent disaster. Organizations need these critical competencies and cannot survive without them, and that is why organizations need leaders.

You know you are credible when the organization senses its need and then looks for a leader, and this leads them to you. But this brings us to an important point. No leader is competent to fill every leadership position in every organization. Leadership involves many generic competencies, but the most crucial are specific to the organization, and sometimes even to a particular part within it.

Retired military leaders are usually not a natural fit for academic leadership, and the reverse is equally true. Pastors may or may not be a good fit for leadership in a denominational agency. A CEO's strong and effective leadership in one context does not necessarily ensure the same in any other. No leader is competent in all circumstances and contexts, nor do you need to be. You must be competent in the skills and abilities of the leadership role to which you have been called.

Credibility Can Be Earned

There are some leaders who inspire and motivate just by their physical presence. They have rare gifts of personality and character that almost compel others to follow them. Others who aspire to leadership often look to these natural-born leaders and assume that the call to lead is simply beyond their reach.

But keep this always in mind: The most essential element in determining whether others will follow you is your credibility to lead them and to guide the organization to the right future. If you are credible, they will follow. If not, you will never be effective as a leader.

So how is credibility earned?

Part of it has to do with character, as we've discussed, and this dimension of credibility is the leader's life project. But other elements of competence are different. Some positions of leadership require specific educational preparation and academic credentials. It makes little sense to aspire to a leadership position unless you are willing to undertake the studies and preparation necessary to establish such credibility. If you lack the passion for the preparation, you will lack the passion for the leadership responsibilities.

Other positions of leadership require the credibility that comes through experience. Most Fortune 500 CEOs have extensive experience at various levels of their companies, and many have previous CEO experience. There are no newly minted generals or admirals who sit on the Joint Chiefs of Staff. The aspiring leader must be willing to gain that experience the hard way. At the same time, every leader must be ready to be called when least expected.

When I was called to be president of the Southern Baptist Theological Seminary, I had never served as a professor, a dean, or a vice president. I was then editor and chief executive of a newspaper, where I had been dealing in public with the issues that most concerned the seminary and our churches. I was well known as a speaker and preacher. I had extensive experience as an assistant to the previous president of the school, and I had graduated with the PhD degree just four years earlier.

No leadership search firm would have gone first to a thirty-three-year-old who had never held a senior title within a college, university, or graduate school. In fact, they did not come to me first, but eventually the search committee came to me because I had the one most important element of credibility—a firm vision of what the institution was all about, a deep knowledge of the urgent challenges it faced, and a clear strategy to get it moving in the right direction.

Needless to say, my work was cut out for me. I had credibility with the search committee and, soon thereafter, the board of trustees. But as for earning credibility with the rest—the school, the denomination, donors, accreditors, and others—that seemed a Herculean task. I was one of the youngest employees of the institution, and I was now president, chief executive officer, and chairman of the faculty. I had to earn credibility quickly and furiously.

So trust me when I tell you now as I speak almost twenty years later: Credibility can be earned. As a matter of fact, that is the only way you can get it. So get started. In my case, I earned it by showing up prepared, ready to lead, and determined to get the job done.

Credibility Can Change the World

Back in the 1930s, no one would have seen Winston Churchill as a future prime minister of England. This period has been described as his "wilderness years," when his influence was minimal and his reputation largely destroyed. Before this he had been at the center of power, serving as first lord of the admiralty and in a succession of cabinet and leadership posts, including Britain's chancellor of the exchequer.

But as the 1930s arrived, Churchill found himself on the periphery of power, and most had written him off as a prospect for future leadership. He had switched parties—twice, in fact—and was not trusted within the Conservative Party he called home once again. He remained in parliament but was increasingly isolated. He was also growing old.

And yet Winston Churchill understood the times better than anyone else within Britain's elite establishment. He might have been sidelined from leadership, but he had a keen eye on Germany, and he saw the rise of Adolf Hitler and the Third Reich as a dagger soon to be held at Britain's throat.

Britain's establishment, including the senior leadership of Churchill's own Conservative Party, was living in a delusional world. Churchill warned of Hitler's militarism and rearmament of Germany, but the British political class considered Churchill to be the warmonger, not Hitler. Churchill wrote articles and gave countless speeches documenting Hitler's growing menace and his military ambitions. He so irritated Britain's prime minister Stanley Baldwin that Baldwin attempted to subvert Churchill within his own local constituency in order to remove Churchill and his voice from the House of Commons.

Britain was so scarred by the carnage of World War I that its leadership could not imagine a second world war. Baldwin's successor as prime minister, Neville Chamberlain, sincerely believed that he could charm and persuade Hitler. He returned from the Munich conference with Hitler on September 30, 1938, and declared that he had achieved "peace for our time."

Of course, that peace had evaporated within hours of Chamberlain's return. When Hitler invaded Poland just a year later, World War II had begun. Chamberlain's credibility had been destroyed, along with that of almost everyone in the political establishment. Only one man had the credibility to lead Britain as it faced its greatest challenge in centuries, and that was Winston Churchill.

Few leaders on the world scene could serve as such a dramatic example of credibility in action. But even though Churchill had been proven right, when virtually the entire political establishment had been proven wrong, he still had to establish credibility with the British people and with their critical allies, most importantly the United States.

Churchill's remarkable achievement in accomplishing that great goal was central to his goal of saving Britain itself. It also serves as a reminder to every leader that credibility can be earned.

Credibility Can Be Lost

The good news is that credibility can be earned. The bad news is that it can also be lost. Once again, examples on the world stage help us see this process at work. The British political establishment lost credibility when Hitler broke the Munich Pact, and it was only a matter of time before the British government fell. Credibility can be lost by moral failure or by a disastrous misadventure in leadership. President Richard Nixon lost his credibility when his high crimes and misdemeanors became known to the American people. The particulars of his misdeeds (such as the obstruction of justice) were less important to the American public than the general sense that Nixon could not be trusted.

> The good news is that credibility can be earned. The bad news is that it can also be lost.

President Jimmy Carter lost his bid for reelection in 1980 when he lost the credibility to lead through indecisive leadership of the economy and a sense of weakness with the Iran hostage crisis. President Herbert Hoover lost all credibility to lead the nation through the Great Depression.

Leaders in businesses and churches can suffer the same fate, but not every loss of credibility is beyond recovery. Soon after taking office,

President John F. Kennedy was faced with a decision that, as commander in chief, only he could make. His military advisors promised him that the Bay of Pigs invasion should be authorized, assuring the president that there was a high likelihood of success and only a small chance of failure.

What then happened can only be described as one of America's most humiliating moments. We left Cuban freedom fighters to die by the scores because we were unwilling to confront the Soviet Union by allowing air support by the United States Air Force. Coming so early in his term as president, the catastrophe threatened to capsize John F. Kennedy's administration and to ruin his political future. Kennedy's credibility was almost wrecked in the shallow waters of the Bay of Pigs.

But what Kennedy did in response is a textbook lesson in regaining credibility. He took responsibility for the disaster and promised to learn from it. He created a new National Security Council within the White House and made certain that the commander in chief had access to the best military intelligence and advice. When put to the test again, in the Cuban Missile Crisis, President Kennedy more than regained his credibility.

Thankfully, most of us will never face the very real threat of leading when failure means global thermonuclear war. But Christian leaders face the even greater reality that the credibility of our leadership can have eternal consequences. Every single day, the faithful leader must be aware that credibility is the essence of leadership, and that it can be both earned and lost. The effective leader cannot afford to lose credibility—in fact, he needs to stockpile it and build it in reserve.

When the leader enters the room, trust and confidence must enter with him. That is the secret of credibility, and you cannot lead even a Boy Scout troop without it.

Leaders Are Communicators

The Leader's Most Essential Skill Is the Ability to Communicate . . . Over and Over Again

So what do leaders actually *do*? The answer to that question is an ever-expanding list of tasks and responsibilities, but one central duty stands out above all others—the leader communicates.

Actually, the truth is even more dramatic. Leadership doesn't happen until communication happens. The leader may have the most brilliant strategy in his mind, the most breathtaking vision in his sights, and an irrepressible passion in his heart, but if these are not communicated to others, real leadership just doesn't occur.

To be human is to communicate, but to be a leader is to communicate constantly, skillfully, intentionally, and strategically. The effective leader communicates so pervasively that it seems second nature, and so intentionally that no strategic opportunity is ever surrendered.

Many people try to contrast communication with action, as if the two are at odds. But communication *is* action, and the leader will spend more time communicating than in any other activity. The best leaders know that the road to great effectiveness is paved with intentional communications, and the very best leaders are always learning how to be even more effective as communicators.

To lead by conviction is to underline this truth. We lead this way because we are convinced that the right beliefs will lead to the right thinking and eventually to the right course of action. This is the pattern we find in the Bible, and for this reason the church's central responsibility is also to communicate—to teach and preach the gospel. The church is led by those who teach, and taught by those who lead.

So, as a matter of fact, is every powerful organization.

God made us this way and gave us the gift of language for this very purpose. We were created to communicate—to send and receive an almost unceasing flow of information, impressions, symbols, and, most important of all, *words*.

Words are the priceless currency of communication. The most effective leaders are collectors and connoisseurs of words. They polish and perfect the deployment of specific words for greatest effect. They know that words are powerful when memorable and delivered with conviction. They know that Mark Twain was right when he said that the difference between the almost right word and the right word is "the difference between the lightning bug and the lightning."

Let's be honest. One essential requirement of leadership is the ability to talk, and to talk well. While the leader's responsibility to talk is most often associated with public speaking, the actual work of leadership requires the ability to talk in any number of different contexts, and to master written expression as well.

Where Does It Start?

Write this down: If a leader has to look for a message, his leadership is doomed. Leaders communicate because they cannot *not* communicate, and their message flows out of them as naturally as a geyser releases its energy. This is the essence of convictional leadership. The message flows out of your deepest convictions and most passionately held beliefs. The most powerful leaders are those whose beliefs function like an engine of meaning—pushing out words and messages and compelling communication.

Have you ever noticed how much easier it is to listen to a speaker who knows what he or she believes and stands ready to speak out of those convictions? This is certainly true in the realm of political leadership. It is downright painful to listen as some officials or candidates seem to be searching for a message as they stand behind a podium or answer questions from the press. Compare that with Margaret Thatcher, Ronald Reagan, or Franklin Delano Roosevelt. They were natural communicators, gifted with remarkable abilities. But any number of others had the same gifts, some in even greater measure. What set those leaders apart was the strength and vitality of their message, which came right out of their most passionate beliefs.

> **If a leader has to look for a message, his leadership is doomed.**

I once had the opportunity to meet Senator George McGovern and hear him speak. This event came almost forty years after McGovern lost to Richard Nixon in the landslide election of 1972. McGovern won only Massachusetts and the District of Columbia. He was later to quip, "Ever since I was a young man, I wanted to run for the presidency in the worst possible way—and I did."

Senator McGovern and I are far apart when it comes to many (maybe most) matters of national policy, but I thoroughly enjoyed listening to the senator speak that day. It was impossible *not* to listen to him, and to do so intently. McGovern may have lost in a landslide, but he never lost his convictions. Almost forty years after his defeat, he was still coming out swinging, delivering a stump speech filled with his convictions.

The same pattern holds true in any other context of leadership, ranging from the military and business to education and the church. Leaders who seem to be grasping for a message can cause downright panic in the organization.

If you don't have a message, don't try to lead. If you do have a message, your task is to communicate it effectively. Once you begin to communicate and connect, leadership just happens. And here is the good news—the art and craft of communication can be learned. The truly transformative leader is always learning how to communicate more effectively and how to enjoy it even more as leadership matures.

The Hallmarks of Powerful Communication

Convictional leadership begins with a commitment to truth and a relentless desire to see others know and believe that same truth. But communication is a form of warfare. The leader is always fighting apathy, confusion, lack of direction, and competing voices. The wise leader understands this warfare and enters it eagerly.

The effective leader aims for three essential hallmarks of powerful communication. The first is *clarity*. Although almost no one sets out to be a confusing communicator, many end up becoming just that. The more they speak, the more they confuse. They get wrapped up in phrases and messages and ideas and create fog rather than light. Powerful communication requires clarity, first of all.

Winston Churchill once explained the compelling force of his messages by pointing to the power inherent in a single English sentence. The goal of communication is not to impress but to convey meaning and purpose. The best leaders lean constantly into clarity, refusing to allow their messages to be entangled in clouds or trapped in a jungle of words.

Perhaps the greatest example of this principle comes from the apostle Paul, who explained himself to the Corinthians like this:

> And I, when I came to you, brothers, did not come proclaiming to you the testimony of God with lofty speech or wisdom. For I decided to know nothing among you except Jesus Christ and him crucified. And I was with you in weakness and in fear and much trembling, and my speech and my message were not in plausible words of wisdom, but in demonstration of the Spirit and of power, so that your faith might not rest in the wisdom of men but in the power of God.
>
> 1 Corinthians 2:1–5

Paul was a master of clarity, and he knew that his message must point directly to Christ and his atoning work. He refused to use rhetorical tricks or to rely on eloquence. He set the standard for Christian leaders by preaching the gospel with breathtaking clarity.

Whatever our position of leadership, the Christian leader must follow this same principle. We must communicate directly and clearly, and we must avoid cluttering up our own message and thus confusing those we are called to lead. Clarity is not only advisable, it is essential. The second hallmark is *consistency*. The effective leader knows to communicate with unvarying consistency. If you do not, inconsistencies will weaken or fatally compromise your leadership. Convictional leadership requires a constant and consistent message, no matter the context, the audience, or the occasion . . . and no matter what may come. Powerful leaders are known for showing up with the same message, the same convictions, and the same principles every time they appear. A reputation for inconsistency betrays a lack of conviction, and a lack of conviction is the nullification of leadership.

> A reputation for inconsistency betrays a lack of conviction, and a lack of conviction is the nullification of leadership.

Like so much that is involved in leadership, this requires the leader to listen to those around him and to make certain that the message coming from the leader is truly consistent. We all need colleagues and friends who can listen to us and help us to ensure consistency of thought and of message. But at the end of the day, the leader bears this responsibility alone, and this points to the third hallmark of powerful communication, *courage*.

No one said it was going to be easy. Leadership is a risk, and those who are afraid to take that risk need to stay far away from the responsibilities of leadership. Communication requires courage for the very simple reason that, if your convictions mean anything at all, someone will oppose you. If opposition to your ideas and beliefs offends you, do not attempt to lead. Every leader knows the experience of rejection and opposition. You must prepare for it, expect it, and deal with it when it happens.

A few years ago I was invited to speak at one of the nation's most illustrious universities. The invitation was from the Ivy League school's president, who was trying to deal with a campus crisis brought about by a raging controversy over the question of religious belief in American public life. I accepted the invitation and prepared my speech, fully aware of the fact that the campus was already deeply divided and that the event would be shrouded in controversy. The other speakers and I were advised of the security protections in place for the event.

As I began my speech, I noticed something that I had never experienced before. One of the world's most famous authors, a winner of the Nobel Prize, was sitting in the front row, holding his head in his hands in disapproval as I spoke. I had seen people scowl as I spoke and even shake their heads in disagreement. But a Nobel laureate with his head in his hands in the front row? That was a first for me.

I quickly realized that this was why I was at the event, and why I simply had to say what I came to say. I had a job to do and a message to communicate, and this message was drawn from my deepest and most cherished convictions. At that moment I realized once again that leadership is a "do or die" calling. Everything I stood for would have been compromised had I backtracked when I saw that man with his head in his hands.

Every leader has these moments, but the courage required for leadership and for the risk of communication is usually the everyday courage required to get up in front of people and expose yourself and your message to the scrutiny of others. If this seems too daunting, then follow. Do not aspire to lead.

Say It Again, and Keep on Saying It

Finally, the effective leader understands that the message has to be communicated again and again and again. If you listen to the most influential leaders, you will see that they repeat themselves over and over. This is not the monotonous repetition of a single-track mind, but the intentional, symphonic, and strategic repetition of central truths, cherished beliefs, common strategies, and shared principles.

Those closest to you will hear you say the same things repeatedly. Your closest associates may be able to lip-synch some of your lines and expressions. You cannot worry about that. Your charge is to lead, and this means knowing that you will have to show up again and again with the same clear, consistent, and courageous message.

I once had the opportunity to spend a good part of a day with a man who worked closely with Ronald Reagan. He told me that President Reagan actually had only one speech—he just added different introductions and conclusions to it. This was an overstatement, of course, as a review of the president's speeches will reveal. But at the same time, there is something profoundly true about this man's point. When a true leader shows up, we already know what he is going to say.

Leaders Are Readers

When You Find a Leader, You Find a Reader, and for Good Reason

As a general rule, clichés are to be avoided. The statement that leaders are readers is an exception to that rule. When you find a leader, you have found a reader. The reason for this is simple—there is no substitute for effective reading when it comes to developing and maintaining the intelligence necessary to lead.

My guess is that you know this already. After all, you are reading this in a book. In all likelihood, your desk has a stack of books, magazines, and journals waiting to be read, and your briefcase is filled with reading materials. Leadership requires a constant flow of intelligence, ideas, and information. There is no way to gain the basics of leadership without reading.

Leaders read even when no one else seems to be reading. Author Mary Higgins Clark was once a flight attendant with Pan American. Clark noted that on flights at that time almost everyone on the plane was carrying a book. "Now," she says, "everyone seems to be carrying a computer or looking at the television."

Everyone, that is, except leaders. The explosion of books and articles on leadership is one signal that leaders are avid readers and eager consumers of the written word. Leading by conviction demands an even deeper commitment to reading and the mental disciplines that effective reading establishes. Why? Because convictions require continual mental activity. The leader is constantly analyzing, considering, defining, and confirming the convictions that will rule his leadership.

The Care and Feeding of Conviction

Convictions are the product of both head and heart. There is an emotional component to belief, as well as an intellectual component. The Christian tradition speaks powerfully of the commitment of belief as a matter of the heart. Christian convictions take possession of our heads and hearts through Christian teaching and the preaching of God's Word. As a matter of fact, most of us gain our most fundamental convictions in just this way—we hear them, see them to be truly revealed in the Bible, and then believe them.

> Convictions require continual mental activity.

But growing Christians do not just listen—they also read. We can gain a great deal from what we hear, but auditory learning has its limitations. The experience of reading words in print is different from the experience of hearing words spoken. As a matter of fact, most of us have had the experience of reading a text that was first read aloud to us and noting how much we missed by merely hearing it.

Leaders know that reading is essential, as it is the most important means of developing and deepening understanding. That is why leaders learn to set aside a significant amount of time for reading. We simply cannot lead without a constant flow of intellectual activity in our minds, and there is no substitute for reading when it comes to producing this flow.

Convictions are honed and enriched through reading, especially when that reading is filtered through the kind of worldview analysis that Christian leaders must develop and deploy. The careful reader is not reading merely to receive data. The leader learns to invest deeply in reading as a discipline for critical thinking.

How to Read

You are already a reader, but how can you hone that skill to your greatest benefit? Reading is like any other skill—most people are satisfied to operate at a low level. For some, the skill of reading seems to come naturally, while others have to work hard to develop it. The key is to keep improving over a lifetime.

Your first concern is to read for understanding. If you don't, reading will add little to your life and leadership abilities. Before you start to read a book, ask certain questions about it. What kind of book is it? Most readers find the experience of reading fiction to be very different from the experience of reading a treatise on economics. How dense is the content? Some books and articles can be read very quickly, while others take much longer. What do you need to know about the author? What is the purpose and subject matter of the book? How did it end up on your reading list?

Develop your own rules and habits for reading, and don't worry about what some teacher told you years ago. I like to start with the book's cover and table of contents. The cover of a book used to be mostly for its protection, but now it contains a significant amount of information, ranging from a short biography of the author to the identification of the publisher. The table of contents, if well constructed, is like a map of the book. Reading is much more effective if the reader knows where the book is headed.

You should read a book or article only for what it is worth. If you find that the book is not contributing to your life and leadership, set it aside. The world is filled with books and other reading material. And in this respect, time is more valuable than money. Is the book making you think? Do you find that it is sparking new thoughts and reflections as you read? If so, read on. If not, set it down and move on.

Learn to read critically. Reading is not merely an exchange of information and ideas. It is a conversation between the author and the reader. Think of reading as a silent but intensive conversation. As you read, ask the author questions and filter the book's content through the fabric of your convictions. Argue with the book and its author when necessary, and agree and elaborate when appropriate.

Treat the book as a notepad with printed words. In other words, write in your books. Make the book your own by marking points of agreement and disagreement, highlighting particularly important sections of text, and underlining and diagraming where helpful. Unless your specific copy of the book has some historical or emotional value, mark it up with abandon.

The activity of marking your books adds tremendously to the value of your reading and to your retention of its contents and your thinking. I can go back to a book I read a half century ago and reenter my experience of reading that book for the first time. My notations and remarks make this possible. Often when I reread a book I read many years ago, I am struck by how I read it somewhat differently now, marking different passages and asking the author different questions.

Reading critically also means evaluating the author's credibility and clarity of thought. Does the author have the credentials and authority to make these arguments or to present this information? Do the arguments meet the tests of truthfulness, honesty, and relevance? Are claims backed up with credible evidence and argumentation? These are all crucial questions any reader should ask of a book. A couple more include: What is the author's purpose in writing this book? What do I hope to get out of the experience of reading this book?

Should you read slowly or quickly? That depends on your reading style and the nature of the book. Some readers can read very quickly, retaining information and fruitful thought. Other readers need more time. Wherever you fall on this spectrum, keep reading and developing the skill of reading over your lifetime. Similarly, some books can be read comparatively fast, while others take more time. A friend of mine refers to some books as "bathtub reading"—light reading that can be done just about anywhere and anytime. Other books, however, require the kind of deliberate and careful reading that can tax the mind and memory. Slow down for books like these.

When possible, read for enjoyment. Novelist James Patterson wisely advises parents to determine what kind of reading their children enjoy, and then let them grow in the enjoyment of that reading. Once they love the experience of reading, their appreciation can be broadened to other categories of books. Children who never experience enjoyment in reading seldom become good readers. The same principle applies to adults. We can train ourselves to enjoy reading.

What to Read

Think of reading like you think of eating. In other words, pay attention to your diet. For the Christian, the highest reading priority is the Word of God. Our spiritual maturity will never exceed our knowledge of the Bible, which is an especially urgent principle for Christian leaders. In terms of other reading, Christian leaders should read serious Christian books—books that contain spiritual health and deep thought. At the top of this list should be classics of Christian thought and devotion.

Along these lines, place a priority on reading old books. C. S. Lewis, who certainly wanted people to read contemporary books, nevertheless advised readers to feed deeply on old books. "Naturally, since I myself am a writer, I do not wish the ordinary reader to read no modern books. But if he must read only the new or only the old, I would advise him to read the old." Lewis explained that older books have proved themselves to be worthy by their survival and influence. That is good advice.

> **Think of reading like you think of eating. In other words, pay attention to your diet.**

The leader's reading diet should include books covering a range of subjects, though most of us will invest first in those books that are most relevant to our work and mission. Expanding from there, the leader should learn to consult book reviews and notices in major newspapers, magazines, and online sources. Of course, many of the books that will mean most to us are recommended by friends. When leaders gather, books are usually part of the conversation.

Should leaders read fiction? This is where many leaders admit uncertainty, but the answer is surely yes. Leaders need to read fiction for enjoyment, for learning, and for context. Fiction is important because it allows the reader to enter into the times, life, and mind of someone else. Novels and short stories are powerful units of narrative, telling a story with compelling force. While enjoying the story, leaders are also learning how to improve their own narrative presentation and communicative ability.

The same is true, to a considerable degree, with the best nonfiction. Leaders are ravenous consumers of historical biographies. Their natural instinct is to learn about leaders of the past in order to embrace their strengths and avoid their weaknesses. But the wise leader will range across the waterfront of disciplines, from history and economics to current events and politics. Add to this the expanding number of business and management titles published each year. No leader can read all of these, of course, but the best of the lot should be on the leader's reading list.

What about newspapers, magazines, and newsletters? The capable leader knows that these are important as well. Even as printed newspapers suffer from circulation losses, they remain extremely influential and informative. As a general rule, leaders who want to stay on top of current events should read the *New York Times*, *Wall Street Journal*, and *USA Today*, along with their local newspaper. The *New York Times* and *Wall Street Journal* are the most influential newspapers in the United States, and they generally balance each other in editorial slant and coverage. Both offer comprehensive news coverage with the quality of analysis that leaders need—even as wise leaders take the editorial bias of the newspapers into account. *USA Today* offers a quick summary of the news. Your local newspaper is your best guide to local affairs. These papers can be read quickly or slowly, depending on time and interest. But you can count on this—the nation's most influential leaders in business, academia, politics, entertainment, and the media read these papers daily.

If newspapers represent the first level of report and analysis, then magazines, journals, and newsletters represent the second. The newsweeklies and major intellectual magazines are extremely influential in terms of popular culture. The leader should plan a reading diet that will include exposure to these materials, but keep in mind that most magazines will grow old and out of date quickly. In addition to keeping up with the news, leaders will also learn communication and writing skills from the best magazines and journals. The writing in these periodicals tends to be fresh and lively, intended to draw and keep the reader's attention. That is the wise leader's concern as well.

When to Read

There will never be enough time to read all that you want to read, or even all that you think you *ought* to read. Just keep reading. Set aside segments of time devoted to reading and grab every spare minute you can find. Keep reading materials with you at all times, or at least close at hand. I often find that travel, though robbing me of time in other respects, gives me segments of time to read. Some books can be read in a flight segment or two. You will know your best reading style, so foster habits that will maximize your reading and its value.

Keep a stack of books ready for reading, and take a couple with you as you travel. Keep one in your business case for access when you are stuck in an airport or a doctor's office.

When possible, read when you can retain and think most productively. For some people, this is the early morning, for others late at night. Certain times of the year offer good opportunities for reading, such as vacations and holidays. I have found it helpful to plan reading projects. Each year, I plan two or three of these, intending to pursue understanding on a specific issue or area of knowledge. Develop a short list of books in an area, and work your way through them. You will be amazed at how much you can cover in a year.

I also advise dividing your reading plan into three categories. First, books you *must* read. Second, books you *should* read. Third, books you *want* to read. Given a bit of honest thinking, you will have a good idea of how this breaks down for you. Once you have this structure in mind, you can plan the stewardship of your reading time accordingly.

What About Digital Reading?

For some years now we have been warned that the book, specifically the printed book, is soon to be extinct. Don't believe it. The printed book will survive for many years to come. Nevertheless, the arrival of digital reading devices should be celebrated for what they can add to a leader's reading. I read in digital form on electronic readers every week. Some books can be read well in this way, while others are more difficult. The new e-readers will not replace the printed book any time soon, but they are incredible reading technologies on their own, allowing you to carry hundreds of books in your hands, access millions of books at an instant, and have these books constantly available.

More and more, leaders will find such e-reading to come naturally. At the same time, there is nothing like the physical experience of reading a printed book. Though most e-readers offer some form of highlighting and notation, the experience is simply not the same as reading with pen in hand.

Read With Discernment

Christian leaders learn to read with discernment drawn from our deepest convictions. Constant worldview analysis comes like a reflex as the leader develops the capacity and skill of spiritual discernment. Test everything you read by viewing it through the lens of biblical truth and your convictions. Know that your most faithful and productive thinking will often come as you are reading from an author with whom you disagree, even as you apply critical thinking and discernment. Those who would *lead* with conviction must *read* with conviction.

The Leader and Power

The Faithful Leader Knows That Power Is Never an End in Itself

When people think of leadership, they often think of power. There's no denying that an effective leader is powerful. At the same time, we instantly recognize that something dangerous has entered the picture when power becomes the focus of attention.

Before we explore the concept further, the word *power* needs to be looked at more closely. While power can be associated with coercion and oppression, it should also be linked to influence and guidance. In a fallen world, power does hold the potential to corrupt. On the other hand, nothing of magnitude can be done without it. We fear leaders who are too powerful and misuse that power, but then we turn around and look for leaders who are powerful enough to solve problems. In other words, there is no escaping power, and there is no way to lead without it. The real issue is what kind of power a leader should possess and how that power is exercised.

Power and the Essence of Leadership

Leaders get things done. Faithful leaders get the right things done in the right way. The essence of leadership is motivating and influencing followers to get the right things done—putting conviction into corporate action. This requires the exercise of power. We can try to call it something else, but it comes down to the fact that the leader is the one who defines the reality, announces the plan, and directs every part of the organization toward the goal. At every stage in this process, power is involved.

But what is the essence of this power? Is it the leader's personality? The personality factor can never be removed from the leadership equation. Every leader is a flesh-and-blood human being with his own personality and public persona. There is no way around this. The faithful leader understands that God created us with distinct personalities and that every personality has something to add to human culture and society. We were not created as automatons. But faithful leaders understand that while they will influence the organization with their personality, they must never allow personality to be the defining mark of leadership.

> **Faithful leaders must never allow personality to be the defining mark of leadership.**

There are two dangers here. The first is the well-known "cult of personality," in which the persona of the leader becomes the hallmark of the organization. Personality cults take over the culture of the organization, with the leader sometimes becoming more prominent than the organization itself. The other danger is that the leader will rely on personality as a substitute for conviction or competence. Personality is important, but it will fall flat when conviction wanes or competence is lacking.

In addition to the power of personality, power also comes from the office the leader holds. This is an absolutely vital aspect of leadership. The leader is invested in office, and the proper stewardship of the power the office commands is crucial.

When I was elected editor of a newspaper at a very young age, I sat down at my desk that first week and tried to figure out what the job was all about. Any confusion was dispelled with the arrival of the deadline for the first edition under my leadership. I realized—all at once—that I was responsible for every single word in that newspaper. I saw the masthead, and there was my name with the title Editor underneath. My whole outlook on life and leadership changed in that instant. I held an office, and my charge was to get the job done. As editor, I could order changes in any article, on any page. But I and I alone would have to answer for every word in that newspaper.

A leader unwilling to exercise the responsibility of office has no business accepting that stewardship. Harry Truman's famous admonition "If you can't stand the heat, get out of the kitchen" applies to every leader. Leaders must keep one truth constantly in focus—the office you hold exists because the organization depends on it. Organizations operate out of countless organizational charts, and nomenclature varies widely, but every organizational structure depends upon the power of office, whether this is honestly admitted or not.

Someone has the responsibility to answer for the organization. Someone has the authority to hire and to fire. Someone proposes a budget and has spending authority. In any organization of size, someone has executive authority. The wise leader knows that the stewardship of office is a matter of highest priority. The health and welfare of the entire institution depends on it. At times, this is the only authority the leader really has.

I found this out the moment I walked onto the campus of the institution I lead after being elected its president. At that point, no one on campus seemed to be impressed with my personality. I had been elected by the board and charged to take the school in a very different direction from where it had been headed for a half century or more. This was not a small course correction. It was a revolution.

Arriving on campus, I quickly determined that all the tools of persuasion and collaboration I prized were useless. They would be crucial once I had my own team in place, but first I had to stare down a powerful faculty and administrative staff and force a complete U-turn of the school's direction. Personality really did not matter at that point. Humanly speaking, I had one (and only one) thing going for me: The board had elected me president, chief executive officer, and chairman of the faculty. All I had was the power of office, and I had to use that power to the fullest.

I look back now at photographs of that skinny thirty-three-year-old the board had elected to such an office, and I shudder. What were they thinking? But if they were thinking that I knew how to use the power of office, they were right. I had learned a great deal before I arrived on campus, but the next few months and years were a crash course in leadership, taken the hard way.

Here is what I learned—the power of office works in two ways. First, it allows leaders to define reality to outside constituencies. The one who holds the office of leadership gets to speak for the organization. Others within the organization can (and often will) have their own say, but the office carries weight and amplifies voice. Wise leaders know this and seize the opportunity to define reality in terms of convictions and mission and truth.

Second, the power of office allows the leader to force change within the organization. Don't get weak knees now. Any leader unwilling to force change is destined for ineffectiveness. The faithful leader uses this power sparingly, but uses it nonetheless. In a healthy organization, this power is always there if needed, but the leader's first job is to use influence and persuasion and focused collaboration to get the job done. When those fail or flag, the leader has to step in and force action.

Oddly enough, most leaders will find that if they steward this power well, the organization actually operates on a high level of trust and effectiveness. This may be counterintuitive, with many people assuming that any use of the power of office to force change will be resisted. But this is a false assumption. The truth is that people within an organization feel most secure when the leader leads. They know that their own hard work will not be thwarted by institutional lethargy. They can have confidence that, at the end of the day, the leader who holds that office of trust will force action if necessary.

The Morality of Power

All of life is moral. There is no dimension of life that does not involve moral principles and moral consequences. This is especially true when it comes to leadership, and never more so than when the leader exercises power.

The most sobering thought I often have in the course of a day is that I will make decisions that will impact people's lives. By virtue of the stewardship and leadership invested in me, I have to make these decisions. James 3:1 reminds us that "we who teach will be judged with greater strictness." The same is surely true when it comes to those who lead—since we so often lead by teaching. We will bear a far stricter judgment than those who follow. When it comes to the exercise of power, this is a sober warning.

Clearly, as we discussed earlier in this chapter, the Christian leader must resist the cult of personality. There are so many temptations here, and the line between the right deployment of personality and the disaster of cultic leadership is often very fine indeed. In an increasingly complex culture, personality is one thing people think they can understand. When everything becomes a brand, personality is branded as a product. But while the power of personality can be dangerous, it would be both foolish and dishonest for the leader to claim that leadership can be severed from personality.

Perhaps it is best to think of the power of personality like this: If the leader's main task is to lead by conviction, then the convictions must be more central and prominent than the leader's personality. If the personality looms larger than the convictions, alarms should go off, and they had better be heeded.

Furthermore, the Christian leader cannot succumb to the temptations of ostentation and the glorification of power. As Jesus instructed his disciples, "You know that the rulers of the Gentiles lord it over them, and their great ones exercise authority over them. It shall not be so among you. But whoever would be great among you must be your servant, and whoever would be first among you must be your slave" (Matthew 20:25–27).

This does not fit the leadership advice that comes from Wall Street or the corridors of political power, but it is Jesus' command to his church and his disciples. The Christian leader will respect the role of power in leadership but will never glory in it. The faithful leader will learn the stewardship of power without resorting to the kind of crass calculations offered by modern-day Machiavellis.

The Christian leader will serve by leading and lead by serving, knowing that the power of office and leadership is there to be used, but to be used toward the right ends and in the right manner. Power can never be seen as an end in itself.

Power and Accountability

Friedrich Nietzsche, whose poisonous philosophical influence is still felt today, claimed that the most basic human impulse was a "will to power," and he challenged humanity to embrace that will with abandon. He rejected all moral considerations as forms of weakness and called for the emergence of a great leader who would embody an undiluted will to power on behalf of the people. Twentieth-century history records the genocide and carnage left in the wake of that venomous philosophy.

> The Christian leader will respect the role of power in leadership but will never glory in it.

Christians understand that Nietzsche was on to something. Left to themselves, leaders can and will turn into power-hungry predators. Strangely enough, a considerable percentage of humanity actually seems to want that kind of leadership.

But this is anathema to Christians, who must understand that with power and responsibility must come accountability. A leader without accountability is an accident waiting to happen. I am thankful for a board of trustees whom I do not get to select, but who are elected by the churches of our denomination. We should be thankful for auditors and accountants and imperatives of shared governance.

The difference between a president of the United States and a medieval despot is the fact that a president has to face accountability, most importantly on Election Day. An American president sits atop one branch of government, not all three.

At the same time, there is only one American at any given time who is the nation's chief executive and commander in chief of its military. The health and welfare of the nation depend on the president's fulfilling those responsibilities without apology. But the welfare and safety of the nation also depend upon the limitations placed even on the president of the United States.

The faithful leader understands why this is so and knows that power is both indispensable and deadly. The stewardship of power is one of the greatest moral challenges any leader will ever face.

Leaders Are Managers

Not All Managers Are Leaders, but All Leaders Are Managers

Leadership and management are inseparable, and no effective leader can disparage or neglect competent and efficient management. Leaders who cannot manage quickly become leadership failures. Leaders who leave all management to others are no longer leading the organization, no matter how they may flatter themselves by pretending otherwise. If you think you're above the tasks of management, you're setting yourself up for disaster.

My father managed a large supermarket. As a boy, I would proudly go into his store and see all the activity under his management. I would watch as the cashiers, the butchers, the produce cutters, the bag boys, and the bakers all did their work. At the center of it all was the store manager. When I asked my dad what his job was, he answered directly—to make sure that everything was in place for every employee to do his or her job. Later, when as a teenager I worked in his store, I saw firsthand what that meant. It was a massive organizational responsibility. Indeed, the modern supermarket was only made possible by the invention of management as a profession.

Peter Drucker, the most influential management theorist of modern times, observes that management is a fairly recent development. When Karl Marx wrote *Das Kapital* in the early 1850s, the largest manufacturing company in the world (a cotton mill in Manchester) employed fewer than three hundred people. Larger organizations required the development of management both as a task and as a profession. As Drucker explains, "In less than 150 years, management has transformed the social and economic fabric of the world's developed countries."

Before the rise of management, most people worked as domestic servants, farmers, or manufacturers. Since then, the world has been transformed. As Drucker comments:

> Management has been the main agent of this unprecedented transformation. For it is management that explains why, for the first time in human history, we can employ large numbers of knowledgeable, skilled people in productive work. No earlier society could do this. Indeed, no earlier society could support more than a handful of such people because, until quite recently, no one knew how to put people with different skills and knowledge together to achieve common goals.

That powerful observation underlines exactly what leaders must do—"put people with different skills and knowledge together to achieve common goals." As a matter of fact, that is why leadership exists, and that is why management is essential to what leaders do.

Gary Hamel of the London School of Economics refers to management as "one of humanity's greatest inventions—right up there with fire, written language, and democracy." That is an audacious claim, but a close look at how large organizations have transformed the world lends credence to Hamel's point. Just try doing anything large without management. Management made big corporations possible, but it also allowed for the rise of the modern university, the large church, the modern hospital, the government, and large organizations of all sorts.

So why do so many leaders look down on management?

Leaders Are Managers, but Never Merely Managers

Management got a black eye in the second half of the twentieth century as stereotypes came along like "the man in the gray flannel suit." No one loves a bureaucracy, and no one aspires to be a nameless, faceless bureaucrat. Somehow, even as the modern ideal of leadership was being developed in recent decades, management was disparaged.

Warren Bennis, from whom I have learned much about leadership, is credited with a statement that encapsulates this conventional wisdom: "Managers are people who do things right and leaders are people who do the right thing." There is tremendous wisdom in that statement, especially when we define leadership in terms of conviction. Leaders are the stewards of vision, conviction, beliefs, and strategic decisions. Who cares about the color of the loading dock? Vision requires leadership. The delivery schedule can be left to managers, who need not worry about organizational strategy.

> Leaders absolutely must manage. If not, there will be a disconnect between conviction and operation.

But there is a seductive danger here. While we can agree that many good managers are not really leaders in the visionary and strategic sense, leaders absolutely must manage. If not, the actual mechanics of the organization, its policies and procedures, will be in the hands of others. That means there will be a disconnect between conviction and operation. In other words, the organization will fail.

The attempt to separate leadership from management has led to a host of disasters, and it is easy to see why. Management delivers the goods and determines what the organization actually does. If this is severed from leadership, there is no assurance that the organization will deliver on its mission. As a matter of fact, there is every reason to believe that it will not.

Leaders lead by definition, but they also lead by management. There are certain management tasks that cannot be delegated, or can only be delegated with adequate supervision and oversight.

The Tasks of Management

So what does management actually entail? Once it is defined, the implications for leadership get a lot clearer. As Drucker explains, the fundamental task of management is "to make people capable of joint performance by giving them common goals, common values, the right structure, and the ongoing training and development they need to perform and to respond to change."

> **Management is leadership put into action. The right actions will follow if management has done its job.**

You might say that management is leadership put into action. The right actions will follow if management has done its job.

Elsewhere, Drucker helpfully defines the work of the manager as one who sets objectives, organizes, motivates, communicates, measures, and develops people. These responsibilities underline the importance of management and the imperative that leaders take managerial responsibility with great seriousness.

Going back to Drucker's definition of the fundamental task of management, let's first consider the instillation of common goals. How can leadership happen if the people in an organization aren't trying to move in the same direction? That is a greater challenge than you may think. We often just assume that people working in an organization share common goals, but leaders know not to take this for granted. Common goals are the product of intensive communication, enduring influence, and constant affirmation. People who start out with a common set of goals may drift apart, pushed and pulled by all sorts of events, opportunities, and challenges. Healthy organizations are constantly bringing new people into their workforce. These new people will not embrace common goals by accident. There must be a structure in place to inculcate, define, and affirm these goals throughout the organization.

What about common values? They are the evidence of leadership by conviction. The leader's task is to define and articulate certain values, and then work to see them driven throughout the organization. The leader cannot do this without involving himself in the machinery of the organization.

The next step on Drucker's list is to implement the right structure. Leaders who are unconcerned about structure will not lead for long. A good structure does not ensure success, but a bad structure can ensure failure. This is where Drucker is especially helpful. He defines the right structure as that which allows everyone in the organization to do his or her job. That is a liberating ideal of organization. Leaders must work to make the organization's structure serve, rather than impede, the work. That requires a lot of attention to how the work is actually done, which is to say that a leader who does not know how the work is done cannot possibly lead with effectiveness.

I took the reins at the seminary before I had any substantial experience as a classroom teacher. I had spent years in the academic world, but not as a professor. Trust me, the faculty knew this. I had to learn their world fast, and I had to trust certain capable leaders around me who had that experience. If I did not quickly gain an understanding of that world, I would never have been able to lead the school. Why? Because for the students, and for the churches they would eventually serve, what happens in the classroom is what really matters. I had to immerse myself in measurements such as teaching loads and classroom capacities. I had to enter into their world and understand their work. We were able to revolutionize an institution in a short period of time because we immediately focused on the classroom experience even as the larger tasks of vision, strategic communication, and the care of a constituency grabbed the spotlight.

> **A leader who does not know how the work is done cannot possibly lead with effectiveness.**

Practical Tasks and the Leader's Priorities

Leaders instinctively gravitate to what is most important. This is good, but trouble comes when leaders fail to grasp that some simple and practical tasks can lead, if ignored or neglected, to humiliating disaster.

Consider the budget. I once knew a leader whose only budgetary interest was a thumbs-up sign from the CFO. I get nervous even thinking about that. The budget of any organization is one of the most essential representations of what the organization is committed to doing. The budget sets priorities as it opens some doors and closes others. Budgets send clear signals about commitments and future plans. Anyone able to read the budget can do the math and detect what the organization believes and is committed to accomplishing.

A leader who takes a hands-off approach to the budget isn't leading, but merely suggesting. Effective leaders give intensive personal attention to the budget because that's where the real convictions of the organization show up.

The leader is also responsible for the financial accountability of the organization. A leader who cannot read a financial audit or an accounting spreadsheet is at the mercy of those who can, and that is indefensible. Just consider how many well-intended leaders end up responsible for a financial scandal or a loss of organizational health through financial mismanagement. If you do not know how to read a spreadsheet, learn. You do not need to become an accountant, but you'd better know how to read the data and understand the issues involved.

Personnel policies and structures are also important. Leaders need to give adequate attention to policy details and best practices across a wide spectrum of organizational dimensions. How wide? As wide as the work of the organization you lead.

Organizations change fast as the world changes around us. The effective leader deploys others within the organization to become specialists in the wide array of knowledge necessary to the total work. But that same leader has to make sure that he can at least hold an intelligent, helpful conversation with each of those leaders and managers about their work. The best leaders take this as an intellectual and organizational challenge that they grow to relish and appreciate. After all, our task is to deploy people so that each can do his or her job. In order to do this, we need to know what that job is, and that takes time and attention.

Management by Conviction

Adrian Wooldridge is absolutely right when he refers to "the management theory industry." Every few years some new management fad seems to emerge and dominate the field. The cult of efficiency and "scientific management" of the early twentieth century gave way to "management by objective" as the century drew to a close. A host of other theories can be added to these, each offering its own insights.

The effective leader learns from these theories without embracing any one of them as the sum and summit of the management task. Some new theory will shortly come along, displacing the last with a tidal wave of books, seminars, and attention.

Management by objective, usually credited to none other than Peter Drucker, was probably the most lasting of these theories. After all, who can manage without objectives? The problem is that objectives can be wrong.

Management by conviction is not a theory, just a commitment. That commitment means that the leader exercises management so that the convictions of the organization are honored, perpetuated, communicated, and put into combined action.

As the apostle Paul commanded Timothy, "What you heard from me in the presence of many witnesses entrust to faithful men who will be able to teach others also" (2 Timothy 2:2). Leadership—and management—begins and ends in conviction.

Leaders Are Speakers

Leaders Give Voice to Conviction and Mobilize Hearts and Minds With a Message

In the beginning was the voice. Long before the advent of widespread literacy, the spoken word ruled in human communication. Now humanity seems to be returning to reliance on oral communication. This will come as no surprise to leaders, who know that the ability to speak with power and persuasion is central to their task.

Speech is the currency of great leadership. People expect to hear the human voice deliver a message, explain events, channel enthusiasm, and mobilize others for action. Most of all, we like to hear a story told well by one who relishes its telling.

The call of public speaking produces fear in many people, but leaders overcome this fear in order to accomplish their task. Leaders are speakers. Americans, even more than the British, flocked to see the 2010 film that I referenced earlier, *The King's Speech*. As a student of both history and leadership (and an admitted Anglophile), I was eager to see it. I knew that King George VI had been afflicted since boyhood with a severe case of what was then called stammering, and that he had exerted heroic efforts to overcome this affliction in order to function as king. This was not just to fulfill formal duties. Within his own father's lifetime, most of the historic monarchies of Europe had fallen. Britain possessed a great empire that was held together, in more than a merely theoretical way, by the person of the monarch. Meanwhile, Britain faced the deadly foe of Adolf Hitler and the Nazi menace. If the king could not speak, the monarchy would be wounded, perhaps mortally, and the British people would be denied the unifying function fulfilled by the king's voice.

Interestingly, the invention of radio had made this necessity all the more pressing. In the film, King George V, representing the height of monarchial dignity, says to his son, the future George VI,

> In the past all a king had to do was look respectable in uniform and not fall off his horse. Now we must invade people's homes and ingratiate ourselves with them. This family is reduced to those lowest, basest of all creatures. We've become actors!

George VI describes the agony of his situation by declaring,

> If I'm king, where's my power? Can I form a government? Can I levy a tax, declare a war? No! And yet I am the seat of all authority. Why? Because the nation believes that when I speak, I speak for them. But I can't speak.

Of course George VI did overcome his stammering, and he was able to speak. He was never a polished orator, but the weight of his responsibility forced him to overcome what would have incapacitated many others. And he was right—the British people did believe that when he spoke, he spoke for them.

That is a central principle of leadership. When leaders speak, we speak for the movement, the organization, the company, the congregation, or the institution we lead. If communication is central to leadership, speech is central to communication. Oddly enough, it is even more so now. Just consider how Steve Jobs reinvented the product-release press event. Look to any candidate for major public office and consider the array of microphones cast in his or her face. The digital revolution has made the ability to deliver a spoken message even more important than before, with constituencies, customers, and congregants expecting 24/7 access to your message in your voice.

The Conviction to Lead Is the Conviction to Speak

Convictional leadership requires the communication and transmission of conviction through the leader's voice. At times this function is conversational. More often than not, given the size and complexity of modern organizations, this requires a speech delivered before more than a handful of people. As mentioned in the previous section, some individuals are invigorated by this responsibility, while others are intimidated by it. Let's be honest—if you are truly unable or unwilling to stand up in front of people and speak with conviction, you are not called to the role of leadership. There are other roles of equal worth and dignity, but leadership means speaking, and effective leaders learn to speak with greater skill and ability as they mature in the leadership role.

No one is more boring than a speaker who has no convictions.

Once again, conviction is key. Audiences thrive on convictional messages, and deep beliefs are the engines of their own communication. No one is more boring than a speaker who has no convictions, or who is unsure what those convictions are, or who lacks confidence that those convictions are of transformative importance. In contrast, no form of communication can exceed the spoken word in terms of transmitting and communicating passion and conviction.

At times, a speech can make the difference between war and peace, life and death, tragedy and triumph. I love to read speeches that changed history. One of the greatest of all time was given by another English monarch, Queen Elizabeth I. She spoke to her assembled troops gathered at Tilbury in 1588 as the nation anticipated the disaster of invasion by the Spanish armada. Elizabeth knew that her troops were horribly outnumbered, and so did they. The army also believed it was weakened by the fact that the monarch was a woman, and there were fears for

Elizabeth's personal safety. The queen ignored those warnings and rode to the front of her troops on a warhorse, wearing armor. To the army she declared:

> I know I have the body but of a weak and feeble woman; but I have the heart and stomach of a king, and of a king of England too, and think foul scorn that Parma or Spain, or any prince of Europe, should dare to invade the borders of my realm; to which rather than any dishonour shall grow by me, I myself will take up arms, I myself will be your general, judge, and rewarder of every one of your virtues in the field.

A strong wind later blew the Spanish armada to bits on Europe's rocky coastlines, and Elizabeth's army never had to fight the Spanish on British soil. But Elizabeth had won the hearts of her people forever with that speech. It was an exquisite display of leadership and was undoubtedly the greatest speech of Elizabeth's long reign.

Think of Martin Luther King Jr.'s "I Have a Dream" speech, which, over time, changed the heart of a nation. The case can be made that King's speech actually grew in transformative power over the years, influencing a nation long after King's untimely death. Think of Winston Churchill in the throes of World War II, who rallied the British people (and the Americans too) with his convictional oratory and speeches. Edward R. Murrow later explained that Churchill "mobilized the English language and sent it into battle." More humbly, Churchill suggested that the British people themselves had the heart of a lion—"I had the luck to be called upon to give the *roar*."

The Art and Craft of Public Speaking

Most leaders enjoy speaking, but many do not do it well, and their leadership is hampered. Speaking is an art and a craft, not a science. The most effective speakers love language and enjoy telling a tale. They experiment with different ways of using words and sentences, different strategies for constructing messages and talks. Leaders who are good speakers learn to use their voice as an instrument rather than a piece of equipment. They learn how to use humor without becoming comedians;

to arouse emotion without selling out to emotionalism; and to make an audience want more, not less, from the speaker.

Aristotle was perhaps the greatest scholar of speech in the ancient world—and that was a world largely made by speeches. In Aristotle's day, leaders earned the right to lead on the basis of their oratory and little else. Aristotle broke persuasive speech down into three elements: *ethos*, *pathos*, and *logos*. *Ethos* refers to arguments based in the character of the speaker. This form of argument was more common in Aristotle's day than in ours, but concern for the speaker's character remains just as important now. *Pathos* refers to arguments that are intended to produce change by touching the emotions of the hearers. *Logos* identifies arguments designed to persuade by means of logical argument.

Most leaders lean almost exclusively on *logos* in their speaking, and it is easy to see why. We make decisions based on analysis and knowledge, filtered through reason and conviction. When we stand to speak, our first nature is to present our message, our plan, our strategy as the logically correct option. This truly is important, and if we are not certain that our position is right, we had better go back and make sure. Audiences expect logos. That is, they expect a logical explanation and a reasoned presentation. They do want facts, data, and information. But that is not all they want or expect.

Aristotle knew that human beings are more often persuaded by emotional elements. For this reason, the effective leader must work at establishing a connection with the audience's emotions as well as their intellects. People are usually not very hard to understand. They want the security of knowing that leaders are setting an intelligent, reasonable, and responsible course. But they also want to be part of something great, something significant, something that changes lives.

In other words, the effective leader combines *ethos*, *pathos*, and *logos* in every speech, every talk, every presentation, and every message—every time.

If giving a speech seems daunting, redefine public speaking as storytelling. This will help almost any speaker be more effective. People connect to stories, and the best speeches and messages lean heavily into narrative. Leadership, I have argued, is itself narrative. We are telling a story as we lead, inviting others to be part of that story. Public speaking, regardless of the context, is an extension of that principle of leadership. We speak in order to invite others into a narrative that grows out of deep conviction. Our confidence is that this narrative, put into action, will change lives, and sometimes even change history.

Speaking Is Easier Than You Think

If you are called to lead, you are called to speak. But how exactly are you going to do this? Regrettably, many young people now grow up without the forced experience of public speaking, and rarely do any of them receive formal training in the art. Fortunately for me, my schools did expect students to be able to present a speech. When I was around twelve years old, my parents had the bright idea to send me to a local finishing school that met at the yacht club on Thursday nights. We were not the yachting type, and I felt as out of place as a seventh grader could feel. Nevertheless, I had to learn certain social graces that have served me well, and it exposed me to early experiences in "elocution," or public speaking. It sounded dangerously like "electrocution" to me.

Later, I became a Boys State speaker at age sixteen, and then a campaign worker in political campaigns. I also started teaching Bible studies at age sixteen and the next year preached my first sermon. There has hardly been a week since that I have not had a significant speaking responsibility—now usually several a week. But I am still learning, and I want to be learning with every speech or sermon or message I give until my last.

> **If you are called to lead, you are called to speak.**

I follow a simple process as I get my speech, and myself, ready for the occasion. *First, know what you want to say.* If you do not know what you want and need to say, don't speak. It is just that simple. Any effective and worthy speech begins with the speaker desiring to share a message—and the speaker, above all else, must know what that message is. This is where convictional leadership rescues the leader from the lack of something to say. The convictional leader always has something to say, and that message is the expression of deep beliefs, the very beliefs that brought the organization into existence and give it a reason for being. The leader times, defines, and isolates certain convictions for emphasis, but the entire body of conviction arrives when the leader arrives. Knowing what you want to say drives the entire process of the speech, from conception to delivery. Once you know what you want to say, the rest follows naturally.

Second, know your audience. You need to know the anticipated size, composition, and expectations of the listeners. Your convictions remain constant, but your mode of speaking will vary. You will speak to a group of new members quite differently than you will speak to a room of veterans who have been with you for decades. If the audience will be highly conscious of the time, you had better know this—and get to the point quickly. If you are speaking during a meal, there are particular considerations. For one thing, you will have to be more interesting than the food!

Over time you will develop certain intuitions and the ability to read an audience as you speak. In every case, try to get as much information up front as you can and plan accordingly. This will make you more effective and your audience more comfortable and receptive.

Third, outline your message. The outline is like a road map for your speech. You are not enslaved to it, but it is essential to your strategy for presenting your message. The outline does not have to be complicated or elaborate, but it does need to flow from one major point to another, with data, information points, and emphases clearly identified.

Fourth, frame your presentation. The frame is the big picture into which your message is set—the narrative into which this speech finds its purpose and meaning. You are delivering this message because it fits within your larger leadership mission and agenda, and within the larger strategy for your organization. By framing your message, you put it within this context and strategy while keeping in mind the reason you were asked to speak. Someone invited or summoned these people into this room to hear you. Why? Every speech, sermon, or talk exists to serve some larger purpose. Know what that is, and frame the message to serve that purpose.

Fifth, punctuate and illustrate. By punctuate, I do not refer to the mechanics of punctuating sentences. I mean you must insert particularly powerful and memorable content into your message in order to drive home certain truths, points, and convictions. You can punctuate with your voice, with your language, and with your speaking cadence. Most importantly, punctuate with stories and illustrations that truly fit your message and its points. The best speakers illustrate so well that the audience actually begins to imagine being in the story and participating in the narrative. Punctuation and illustration do not drive the message, but they do drive the message home.

Sixth, get yourself ready. Do whatever you have to do to be ready. Do you need quiet time? Then arrange for it. Do you speak best right out of conversation? Then surround yourself with people before you speak. Do what you need to do to get yourself mentally and physically ready for the speaking event. Then pray that God will use you and your message to his glory. Pray that the people you are addressing will receive truth and ignore error. Then go speak, and let the message find its audience.

Seventh, speak like you mean it. Deliver your message with confidence and zeal, letting your audience know how much you believe what you are saying and how much you want them to believe along with you. Speak the language of conviction, using every appropriate form of argument and explanation that serves your purpose.

Eighth, tell the audience what to do. Many speakers forget or neglect this essential step, leaving the audience informed and emotionally moved but absolutely unsure what to do about it. Do not end your message without an action plan that fits the message. Don't leave your audience asking, "Okay, now what?"

Effective leaders know to develop a feedback loop. Most people will tell you they enjoyed your message, even when they really didn't (or, even more commonly, when they are not sure why it mattered). Develop a feedback loop of those who will tell you the truth—and know that the truth may take a while to come out. Learn from it . . . and keep on speaking with conviction.

Finally, one of the best insights into the art of speaking I have ever found came in the form of an admonition spoken to the late Senator

Hubert H. Humphrey by his wife, Muriel. "Hubert, to be immortal you don't have to be eternal." Applied to public speaking, truer words have seldom been spoken. This chapter is written for leaders in any context. Pastors and preachers will understand that preaching shares much in common with other forms of public speaking, but it also stands out in one urgently important aspect. Preaching is the exposition of a biblical text, not the invented message of the human preacher. The preacher starts with a specific biblical text, and that text sets the agenda for the message. Preaching God's Word is quite different from delivering any other message. I deal with this at length in my book *He Is Not Silent: Preaching in a Postmodern World*.

Leadership as Stewardship

Leaders Never Lead for Themselves; They Are Stewards in Service of Another

Christians are rightly and necessarily concerned about leadership, but many seem to aim no higher than secular leadership standards and visions. We can learn a great deal from the secular world and its studies and practices of leadership, but the last thing the church needs is warmed-over business theories decorated with Christian language.

Christian leaders are called to convictional leadership, and that means leadership that is defined by beliefs that are transformed into corporate action. The central role of belief is what *must* define any truly Christian understanding of leadership. This means that leadership is always a theological enterprise in the sense that our most important beliefs and convictions are about God. These beliefs determine everything else of importance about us. If our beliefs about God are not true, everything we know and everything we are will be warped and contorted by that false knowledge. This fact should raise warning flags for us as we look to secular culture.

The culture around us has its own concept of God, and it has little to do with the God of the Bible. Out in the fog of modern culture, God has been transformed into a therapist, a benign and indulgent patriarch, and a user-friendly deity. As theologian David F. Wells states so powerfully,

> We have turned to a God that we can use rather than a God we must obey; we have turned to a God who will fulfill our needs rather than to a God before whom we must surrender our rights to ourselves. He is a God for us and for our satisfaction, and we have come to assume that it must be so in the church as well. And so we transform the God of mercy into a God who is at our mercy. We imagine that he is benign, that he will acquiesce as we toy with his reality and co-opt him in the promotion of our ventures and careers.

In the aftermath of this crisis in the knowledge of God, many essential truths have been eclipsed or lost entirely, and one of those truths is the principle of stewardship.

The Sovereignty of God and the Stewardship of Leaders

In the secular world, the horizon of leadership is often no more distant than the next quarterly report or board meeting. For the Christian leader, the frame of reference for leadership is infinitely greater. Our leadership is set within the context of eternity. What we do matters now, of course, but it also has eternal consequences, because we serve an eternal God and we lead those human beings for whom he has an eternal purpose.

But the most important reality that frames our understanding of leadership is nothing less than the sovereignty of God. Human beings may claim to be sovereign, but no earthly leader is anything close to being truly sovereign. In Daniel 4 we learn of Nebuchadnezzar, king of Babylon, one of the most powerful monarchs in human history. God judges Nebuchadnezzar for his arrogance and pride, and he takes Nebuchadnezzar's kingly sovereignty away from him. Later, after a humbling lesson, God restores Nebuchadnezzar to his former greatness. Now, if your sovereignty can be taken away from you, you are not sovereign.

After all this happens, Nebuchadnezzar speaks of the lessons he has learned about who is truly sovereign, and he testifies that sovereignty belongs to God alone, stating that "his dominion is an everlasting dominion, and his kingdom endures from generation to generation" (Daniel 4:34).

Like Nebuchadnezzar, today's Christian leaders know that God is sovereign, and we are not. But what does it really mean to affirm God's sovereignty as Christian leaders?

It means that God rules over all space and time and history. It means that he created the world for his glory and directs the cosmos to his purpose. It means that no one can truly thwart his plans or frustrate his determination. It means that we are secure in the knowledge that God's sovereign purpose to redeem a people through the atonement accomplished by his Son will be fully realized. And it also means that human leaders, no matter their title, rank, or job description, are not really in charge.

> The sovereignty of God puts us in our place, and that place is in God's service.

The bottom line is this: We are merely stewards, not lords, of all that is put into our trust. The sovereignty of God puts us in our place, and that place is in God's service.

The Steward: The Real Meaning of Servant Leadership

The biblical concept of a steward is simple. A steward is someone who manages and leads what is not his own, and he leads knowing that he will give an account to the Lord as the owner and ruler of all.

Stewards are entrusted with responsibility. Indeed, stewards in the Bible are shown to have both great authority and great responsibility. Kings had stewards who administered their kingdoms—just think of Joseph as Pharaoh's steward in Egypt. Rich citizens hired stewards to serve as what amounted to chief executive officers of their enterprises—consider the parable Jesus told about the wicked steward in Luke 16:1–8.

Paul describes ministers as "stewards of the mysteries of God" (1 Corinthians 4:1), and Peter spoke of all Christians as "good stewards of

God's varied grace" (1 Peter 4:10). Clearly, this is a concept that is central to both Christian discipleship and Christian leadership. Christian leaders are invested with a stewardship of influence, authority, and trust that we are called to fulfill. In one sense this underlines just how much God entrusts to his human creatures, fallible and frail as we are. We are called to exercise dominion over creation, but not as ones who own what we are called to lead. Our assignment is to serve on behalf of another.

Just think of the leadership failures and crises that regularly fill the headlines. Many, if not most, of these failures originate in the leader's arrogance or overreaching. Stewards cannot afford to be arrogant, and they must quickly learn the danger of overreaching. At the same time, stewards are charged to act rather than stand by as passive observers. Leaders lead, but they do this knowing that they are leading on another's behalf. Leaders—no matter their title—are servants, plain and simple.

A Parable and a Principle

Jesus once told a story of a wealthy man who went on a long journey. Before he left he entrusted his wealth to three servants. To one he gave five units, to another just two units, and to the last he gave only one. Each received "according to his ability," Jesus said. The servant with the five units invested them and made five more. The one entrusted with two units also traded with them and made two more. The servant who had received only one unit dug a hole in the ground and hid it, keeping it safe, he thought.

When the rich man returned, he demanded an accounting. The servant who had received five units but turned in ten was richly praised and rewarded. "Well done, good and faithful servant," said the master. "You have been faithful over a little; I will set you over much" (Matthew 25:21). The servant who had turned two units into four received the same commendation.

The last servant, who hid his master's wealth in the ground, returned what he had been given; nothing lost, but nothing gained. The master rebuked him harshly, calling him wicked and taking his stewardship away. Then Jesus set down this principle: "For to everyone who has will more be given, and he will have an abundance. But from the one who has not, even what he has will be taken away" (Matthew 25:29).

Stewards are given a great responsibility. Those who lead are entrusted with a stewardship that comes ultimately from God and in the end will be judged by him alone. We are given a job to do and the authority to do it. We will shipwreck our leadership if we do not remember that we are stewards, not lords, of all that we hold by trust.

Stewards of What, Exactly?

The knowledge that our calling is a stewardship is both liberating and limiting. We are liberated to lead, but we are limited in our reach. When you think about it, everything we do is bracketed between those two polarities, liberation and limitation.

But of what, precisely, are we stewards? In the first sense, we are assigned a stewardship defined by our calling and responsibility. We serve in defined roles and have job descriptions. At the very least, those realities help us to define our stewardship.

Still, there are several aspects of leadership as stewardship that demand a closer look. The leader is almost always steward of more than any job description can cover. In fact, convictional leaders are called to fulfill a stewardship of breathtaking proportions.

We are the stewards of human lives and their welfare. We have been assigned a task that will affect those we lead as well as untold numbers of others. Leaders are entrusted with those God made in his own image—people whose lives are precious to God and to those who love and depend on them.

We are the stewards of time and opportunity. Few aspects of stewardship can compete with these. Leaders set the pace and determine which opportunities are taken and which are lost. Leaders have to be concerned not only with what their

> Those who lead are entrusted with a stewardship that comes ultimately from God and in the end will be judged by him alone.

organization is doing but with what it *ought* to be doing. There are not many typewriter firms in business today, but almost half of all American adults own a smart phone. Missing an opportunity can spell disaster, and often does.

We are the stewards of assets and resources. The financial health and wealth of your organization may not be the most important measurements of your leadership, but they are hardly irrelevant. The faithful leader knows that organizational assets are to be deployed in the service of the organization and its mission, and are to be invested and managed so that the wealth of the organization grows. This is not because we lead with the ultimate goal of financial growth, but because financial growth is needed if the organization is to fulfill its mission and extend its reach.

We are the stewards of energy and attention. Leaders radiate energy and draw attention, or they cannot lead. Simultaneously, leaders bear the stewardship of the energy of others, determining where and when the organization and its people should, and should not, invest energy. Attention is also a limited resource, a fact that leaders must learn fast or learn painfully. Effective leaders develop the stewardship of organizational attention and spend it wisely.

We are the stewards of reputation and legacy. As we discussed in a previous chapter, just about everyone seems obsessed with branding these days, and brand consciousness is driven deeply into our culture. There is good reason for much of this obsession—we live and lead on the strength of our reputations. Leaders must protect and enhance reputation and legacy, but those concerns are far bigger than mere branding. A product might be rebranded, but an injury to the reputation of a leader or an organization is rarely fixed so easily. Faithful leaders know that our legacy rides on our reputation and the reputation of those we lead.

We are the stewards of truth and teaching. This is the essence of convictional leadership. Leaders are entrusted with truth, with deep beliefs and framing convictions. Those convictions must be taught and retaught, affirmed and reaffirmed, protected and cherished. Otherwise, everything we believe can be lost into confusion, corruption, or worse. As the stewards of truth and teaching, we hold a sacred accountability to perpetuate the very convictions that give life meaning, secure our hope, and summon us and those we lead to concerted action.

It Is Required of Stewards That They Be Found Faithful

Leadership is a trust, and we will answer to God for that trust. There will be many standards and structures of necessary accountability along the way, and leaders answer to an array of judges ranging from shareholders and stakeholders to the press and public opinion. But in the end, all that really matters is the verdict we will receive from the One who invested us with this trust.

The requirement of stewards is that they be found faithful. That's why leadership is only for the brave.

The Leader as Decision Maker

Organizations Expect Many Things From Leaders, Most of All the Trusted Ability to Decide

Human beings are decision makers by nature. History is, in one sense, the record of human decisions, good and bad. Great leaders make big decisions, and the fate of millions of human beings can hang in the balance. Leaders simply cannot avoid making important decisions, and effective leaders stand out because they are both courageous and skilled in making the right decisions again and again.

Leadership is a blend of roles, responsibilities, and expectations. But the one responsibility that often matters most is the ability to make decisions—the right decisions. To be effective, the leader must earn the trust of the organization and its stakeholders—he must be trusted to make decisions and then to take ownership of them. Of course the preponderance of these decisions must be the right decisions, or that trust will erode.

Good decision making has perplexed humanity from its earliest days. You see evidence of this in the Bible when God's people made so many bad decisions over and over again. From the ancient philosophers to the modern scholars of management, many have tried to understand how decisions should be made, proposing various theories along the way. None of these theories ensures success. This is because theories do not make decisions, leaders do.

Consider Dwight D. Eisenhower as he had to decide whether to launch or delay the D-day invasion of Europe. The decision was made all the more excruciating by weather systems that threatened to preclude a successful landing of troops by sea. There was only one slim opening in the weather, and it was not assured. The fate of many nations rested on this decision, and as supreme commander of Allied forces, Eisenhower alone had to make the call. With more than 150,000 troops ready on the ships and landing craft, Eisenhower gave the go signal. We now know that it was the right choice. Eisenhower could not have known that at the time. He simply knew it was the best decision.

> **Indecisiveness is one of history's greatest leadership killers.**

Organizations thrive when leaders make the right decisions, and they fail when leaders make the wrong ones. What is often less obvious is the fact that organizations can suffer worse when leaders refuse to make any decision at all. Indecisiveness is one of history's greatest leadership killers.

So How Do We Make Decisions?

President George W. Bush famously defined the presidency in terms of making decisions. He referred to himself as the decider and titled the memoir of his White House years *Decision Points*. Yet Bush frustrated historians and political scientists because he never explained *how* he made decisions. Perhaps he didn't know. That's not unusual. Many leaders who populate history books made decisions without leaving any evidence of how they made them.

Benjamin Franklin, one of the most ardent advocates for the newly emerged scientific culture, argued that decision making could be reduced to a simple rational process, devoid of emotion or mystery. In essence, he suggested making two columns and then writing down the best arguments for the two clearest options. The column that contained the best arguments overall was, in Franklin's mind, the right decision. Reason is indispensable to decision making, no doubt, but it cannot function alone. After all, we are not creatures of reason alone. Franklin found that his proposed system simply didn't fit many of the decisions he experienced himself making—including the most determinative ones.

Christians understand that human beings, made in God's own image, have been given the capacity to make real decisions and to take responsibility for them. We are also complex creatures with emotions, intuitions, memory, and intelligence all working together. None of us is even fully aware of how we actually make many of the most important decisions of our lives. Does it make sense to say that my wife, Mary, and I decided to fall in love? On the other hand, we did have to decide to get married. Looking back over the years, while I know that my reason was involved, it was not operating alone. I also know that marrying Mary was profoundly the *right* decision.

Leaders make decisions all the time and must be ready to make a decision at any moment. Failure to make a decision paralyzes the organization, and making the wrong decisions can be disastrous. So how does the leader make the best decisions when the decision has to be made?

A Simple Structure for Decision Making

Before making a decision, the leader's preliminary task is to determine if a decision actually has to be made. Odd as this may sound, many organizations suffer because the leader allowed a decision to be made that should never have been decided at all. Moral commitments and the beliefs of the organization necessarily eliminate some decisions from the start. Google's famous motto, "Don't be evil," should, if taken seriously, mean that some corporate options die before any decision has to be made. The leader who allows the unthinkable to be openly considered has sabotaged his organization. Leadership by conviction takes some decisions off the table before the leader gets to work.

Still, the moment of decision comes all too frequently. Six simple steps, taken sequentially, can greatly assist any leader in this task.

First, define the reality. Leaders are deeply invested in reality and must help the entire organization understand the realities that frame its work and future. Defining reality, as Max De Pree, an outstanding leader and author of *Leadership Is an Art*, reminds us, is the leader's first task. So what are the realities that define this particular decision? The leader requires and demands adequate intelligence and information to determine what is at stake. What timetable fits this decision? Whose voices need to be heard? How far and long will its consequences reach?

Second, identify the alternatives. Every decision comes with an array of alternatives, and the leader needs to identify each of them. This is where rigorously honest and intensely creative thinking is necessary. Often the most obvious alternatives are the best alternatives. But at other times, the best decision may be more surprising.

Once the alternatives are honestly identified, those involved in making the decision will have an accurate understanding of the possibilities. At this stage outside advice can be helpful. Leaders are often so close to their organizations that certain alternative actions simply fall beyond their horizons. Even this early in the decision-making process, most leaders find that some alternatives clearly seem more right than others. Sometimes, only one alternative seems right. The temptation is to short-circuit the process, make the decision, and consider the task done. Don't do that. The decision must not be made until the leader is ready—and the leader is not ready yet.

Third, apply analysis. To analyze is simply to take apart. The leader takes the alternatives apart by applying certain tests. Which alternative will serve best, and why? How does each alternative fit within the organization's purpose and mission? Does the organization have the talent and commitment to proceed with a specific alternative? Issues of logistics and budget and personnel and investment are all parts of this analysis, and each organization adds its own set of natural criteria.

Convictional leadership applies the test of belief and conviction at this stage, asking the questions that frame the organization's deepest commitments. Which alternative best fits our beliefs, our convictions, our values? Unless this question rules over all others, the organization will inevitably forfeit or compromise its convictions. Convictional analysis must be rigorous, explicit, and open.

Leadership by conviction means that there will be times when the organization faces an opportunity or option that every financial, numerical, and statistical analysis will suggest is a great decision. In fact, the only reason the organization and its leader should not take this opportunity is because it conflicts or compromises the organization's beliefs and convictions. But that is more than enough to tip the scales. If the option violates conviction, it must be cast aside, no matter the cost. There are some things we just can't do . . . so we won't.

> **If the option violates conviction, it must be cast aside, no matter the cost.**

Fourth, pause for reflection. This is not a stage measured in time, but in mental action. It does not mean delay, it means reflection. Did you leave anyone or anything important out of the equation? Does this feel right to both head and heart? Are you ready to own this decision and stand on it? Given your convictions, will you be proud of this decision in time to come? If so, then press on, and waste no time in delay.

Fifth, make the decision, and make it count. Weak leaders make weak decisions. Effective leaders make solid decisions and see them through. If indecision is a fatal flaw, equivocating afterward is just as deadly. Convictional leaders make the decision, communicate it throughout the organization, and stake their reputations on it.

The leader of conviction not only is willing to live with the decision but fully intends to monogram it with his initials. Consider President John F. Kennedy as he had to make history-determining decisions in the Cuban Missile Crisis. As mentioned earlier, he had been humbled by the Bay of Pigs disaster, but he quickly learned from it (including the hard lesson of which voices around the cabinet table to listen to and which to ignore). President Kennedy's decision to declare a naval blockade of Cuba was technically an act of war, but he handled it with deft diplomacy, and as history now records, his decision was right. Throughout the crisis President Kennedy knew that his name and his name alone would be forever linked to that decision. Powerful and influential men sat around that cabinet table as the world teetered on the precipice of nuclear war, but the commander in chief bore the burden, and he was determined to make the best decision and to live with its consequences. That is leadership in action.

Sixth, review and learn. The stewardship of decision making does not end with the declaration and announcement of the decision. Leaders learn from their decisions and from the process of making them. This is true of good decisions, and even more true of bad ones. Bad decisions can be extremely costly and embarrassing, but they also offer crucial lessons that leaders must not neglect or miss. Some bad decisions will go down in history as expensive lessons in leadership. The leader learns fast, remembers honestly, and moves on.

Winston Churchill was a decision maker driven by conviction, and that is why Britain turned to him at the nation's moment of greatest peril. Churchill was famously indecisive in many personal affairs, frustrating his wife, Clementine. But when it came to affairs of state, Churchill was, as biographer William Manchester described him, the Last Lion. He was resolute, courageous, convictional, and steadfast.

Churchill reminds us that leaders often seem to make their best decisions by what can only be called intuition. His chief of the Imperial General Staff, Field Marshal Alanbrooke, spoke of Churchill's "method of suddenly arriving at some decision as it were by intuition, without any logical examination of the problem." Another said that Churchill made his decisions according to a "zigzag streak of lightning in the brain."

Churchill was usually right, but his decision making, we later learned, was more guided by rational analysis than some of his observers had thought. He is now credited with bringing the British government and military into the modern era of statistical analysis. But at the same time, it was clear that Churchill, like all great leaders, possessed the gift of intuition.

We can be thankful that his decisions were usually right. He did more than any other individual of the twentieth century to save the world from murderous totalitarianisms. But he could also be wrong, and he made some infamously bad decisions. Today's leaders are helped by the honest statement of Churchill's friend F. E. Smith: "Winston was often right, but when he was wrong, well, my God." Even the greatest decision makers leave their scars on history.

I have learned a wealth about leadership by reading history and historical biographies—probably more, in fact, than by reading works explicitly on leadership. Reading President George W. Bush's memoir, *Decision Points*, I was struck by something he said toward the end. He had said something similar to Bob Woodward as the wars in Afghanistan and Iraq were just getting underway: "Whatever the verdict on my presidency, I'm comfortable with the fact that I won't be around to hear it. That's a decision point only history will reach."

I can certainly agree with the former president in his assertion that our reputations, if we are remembered at all here on earth, will be out of our hands once we die, left to the historians. But Christian leaders know that there will be a very different verdict on our leadership and the decisions we make, and that is the verdict of Almighty God.

Leaders have to make decisions day by day. Convictional leaders are determined to make the right decisions, grounded in those convictions. But at the end of the day, all we can do is make the best decisions we can, knowing that the final verdict will not come from shareholders, board members, church members, or even historians, but from God.

"Well done, good and faithful servant" is the verdict for which we strive and hope. The decision to aim for that verdict is one we had better make right now before it is too late.

The Moral Virtues of Leadership

Leadership and Morality Are Inseparable

Leaders are involved in one of the most morally significant callings on earth, and nothing the leader touches is without moral meaning and importance. While the leader shares the same basic moral requirements as everyone else, there are certain virtues that the leader simply cannot do without.

In making us in his image, God created human beings as moral creatures. Our minds are constantly in a moral mode of thinking and reasoning. Our consciences demand attention, and we are continually observing others around us for moral signals.

Our Creator gave us laws, principles, precepts, and commandments that guide us, convict us, and protect us. Christian leaders know to be thankful for the common morality that is revealed in nature and has been recognized in some form in virtually every civilization and culture. We are also thankful for the specific moral instruction given to us in the Bible through the commandments and statutes and laws that frame our Christian moral knowledge.

Furthermore, we must recognize the importance of the moral order represented by the government, which, after all, was also given to us by our Creator in order that we might live in societies of order and peace. If these structures of law and morality did not exist, leadership would be impossible.

But laws and commandments are not enough. Leadership requires the possession and cultivation of certain moral virtues that allow leadership to happen. If the leader does not demonstrate these essential virtues, disaster is certain. Consider certain people who have changed the moral landscape of modern life. When you hear the name Richard Nixon, the first thing that comes to mind is the fact that he became the first (and so far, only) president of the United States who had to resign from office. When you hear of Enron, the first thing we all remember is the spectacular failure and collapse of a major American corporation, at least in part because of fraudulent valuations.

Or think of Bernard Madoff, now sitting in a federal prison in North Carolina, sentenced to 150 years in prison for leading the largest Ponzi scheme in history, with $18 billion defrauded from investors. Madoff defrauded some of the biggest and most illustrious people in the world, and he got away with it for an amazingly long time. But time ran out for Madoff, and the collapse of a vast Ponzi scheme is about as spectacular as the most impressive natural disaster. Madoff is an example of leadership, to be sure. One of the lifers with him in prison wrote about him with great admiration on a prison blog: "He's arguably the greatest con of all time."

Sadly, the same tale of leadership without virtue has meant the collapse of many Christian ministries and churches. The very people who should know the most about the necessity of virtue in leadership can be among the most embarrassing examples of its lack.

Leaders are subject to the same laws, moral principles, and expectations as the rest of humanity, but the moral risks are far higher for them. For that reason, there are certain moral virtues that are especially crucial in the leader's character and life.

Honesty

Truth telling is central to leadership. William Manchester once described the effect Winston Churchill had on Britain when he led the nation at the point of its greatest peril by saying that Churchill "could tell his followers the worst, hurling it to them like great hunks of bleeding meat." Manchester didn't mean that Churchill was either crude or cruel, but that he told his people the truth because the truth alone could save them. Churchill told them the truth about their peril, and then he told them the truth about themselves, giving Britons "heroic visions of what they were and might become."

President Franklin D. Roosevelt demonstrated the same virtue in his Fireside Chats, in which he spoke to Americans of the sacrifices they would have to make and of the price they would have to pay for victory.

One of the greatest temptations that comes to any leader is the temptation to tell something less than the truth. The organizations we lead can fuel this temptation. Our followers would often rather hear a comforting untruth than an uncomfortable truth. Leaders know that telling the truth can be costly and, for that matter, downright awkward. Nevertheless, not telling the truth is a certain recipe for calamity and embarrassment.

A friend of mine, a leader of great courage and virtue, recently had to stand in front of a vast crowd and tell them that the organization he had just been called to lead had been ineffectual for the better part of fifty years. A half century of bloated statistics had obscured the facts, and no one close to the situation had dared to speak the truth for fear of embarrassment, retribution, or even worse. That is a tough job—telling stakeholders that they have all been complicit in hiding the truth from themselves. My friend knew the most important things to know in this situation: first, that telling the truth was simply the right thing to do; and second, that he had to tell the truth in order to clear the way for a better (and more honest) future.

Most of us will never bear a burden of that scale in truth telling, but one of my most important responsibilities when I report to the board of my organization is to point out not only what we are doing well but what we are not doing well. I always try to tell them that they should be asking

> **The leader may have a day out of the office but never a day away from dependability.**

about the projects and programs people are *not* talking about because they are often not talking about them for good reason.

We are always tempted to put our best foot forward, and this is often exactly what we need to do. But we cannot stop there. We must be ready to tell the truth at all times, even when it hurts. If your followers find out that you are not trustworthy, your leadership is undermined, usually fatally.

Dependability

The leader shows up when it matters, every time. A friend recently told me that the thing that mattered to him most as a teenager was the fact that his father always made it to his home ball games, even when he had to get there late due to work. In one game my friend was the final batter in the bottom of the ninth inning, and the game was tied. As he went to bat, he was tempted to look up in the stands to see if his dad was there, but he didn't. He didn't have to. He concentrated and hit the ball, allowing the winning run to score. As he ran back to his teammates he looked up in the stands, and sure enough, there stood his dad, cheering louder than anyone else. That perfectly defines dependability.

The leader is where he needs to be, always. This is not so much a statement of physical presence as it is an affirmation that the leader is always *there* in attention—in charge and ready to lead. The leader may have a day out of the office but never a day away from dependability. The leader is the one individual within the organization that is never, ever totally disconnected from those he leads—and the leader who complains about that is not qualified to lead.

Loyalty

Without loyalty, human endeavors are doomed. Loyalty has fallen on hard times of late, and this is largely due to the breakup of so many of the structures of life that were intended to teach and establish loyalty. Loyalty is hard to maintain in a world of no-fault divorce, broken contracts, and collapsing corporations—but it remains essential. Loyalty has to work in all directions at once. It cannot survive if it is met with disloyalty. If we expect followers, employees, students, members, and customers to be loyal, leaders must be loyal in advance, and consistently so.

Disloyalty is a curse. Great organizations and movements live by the fuel of commitment and loyalty and cannot survive without it. Loyalty starts with fidelity to conviction and the mission of the organization. It radiates out to loyalty toward those who serve that mission and give their lives, skills, and labor to the cause. Finally, it reaches those who are served by the organization or are its customers.

> The movements that make history are those that breed loyalty, and leaders who want to see that kind of loyalty must first demonstrate it themselves.

The movements that make history are those that breed loyalty, and leaders who want to see that kind of loyalty must first demonstrate it themselves. Are the people who follow your leadership afraid that you are only looking for the next opportunity? If so, you can forget loyalty. Do they see you living with less commitment to the mission than you are asking them to have? Congratulations, you just undermined loyalty.

Loyalty grows where it is cultivated and admired. Do you value long service and commitment? If so, admire it openly and express gratitude. Have certain team members demonstrated a particular tenacity and sacrifice for the cause? Celebrate them. When difficulty comes, and it *will* come, loyalty is what we all give to each other and to the cause we serve. That loyalty has to start at the top.

Determination

You cannot lead without tenacity and the unconditional commitment to getting the job done. Technical Sergeant Richard Redding was stringing wire on a telephone pole in Sicily in 1943 as the Allies were engaged in a horrifying battle. Nazi Messerschmitts were strafing at treetop level, but Redding stayed on his pole stringing much-needed communication lines. A voice at the base of the pole yelled up to Redding, asking if he wasn't afraid of those diving fighters. "Yes, sir," he said back. "Then why are you up there?" asked the voice. "Because I am even more afraid of you, sir." The voice asking the question was Lieutenant General George S. Patton Jr. Redding knew of Patton's absolute determination to push the Germans out of Sicily, and that made Sergeant Redding absolutely determined to stay on that telephone pole.

That is how we must lead, and that is how others draw strength from the leader's determination. Slogans, strategic plans, and flow charts cannot deliver determination, only a leader can. Tenacity of purpose is what defines great leadership, and the greater the purpose, the greater the tenacity required.

Humility

Get this straight—leaders will be humble, or they will be humbled. The virtue of humility is deeply rooted in the Christian's understanding of our human frailty. History is replete with examples of those who have been humbled, but this seems to be one of the hardest lessons for leaders to learn.

Part of the confusion lies in false understandings of humility. Humility does not mean that everyone has the same gifts or the same level of giftedness. It does not mean that everyone makes the same contribution to the mission, or that leaders are not invested with a unique level of authority and accountability.

Humility does mean understanding that everything we are and everything we have has come to us as a gift. Leaders have unique abilities, but they received those talents and the ability to develop them as gifts from God, given for the good and welfare of others.

It's not about us—even though we are the leaders given the platform, the position, and the prominence within the organization. The gifts were given to us in order that we might serve others. The minute we forget that and begin to believe our own publicity is the minute we set ourselves up for humiliation.

Humor

Does this virtue surprise you? You do not often see humor listed on a chart of virtues, but it belongs there, and especially for leaders. We are not called to be comedians or humorists, but the effective leader knows that generous, self-deprecating humor is a gift that leaders can give to the people they serve.

Humor humanizes and warms the heart. Those who follow you know that you have weaknesses and foibles, so let them share in the humor you direct at yourself. Humor should never be used at another's expense, but it can be used to make people feel at ease, to relieve tension, and even to affirm humanity. Humor must never be crude or disrespectful, but it can build respect.

I recently saw an example of this when President Barack Obama welcomed former President George W. Bush back to the White House for the unveiling of his presidential portrait. That ceremony is one of America's political traditions, but it meant that Bush and Obama would have to share the stage in the East Room before the watching world. The political tensions were incredible. Obama had run against the record of Bush in 2008, and Bush would be doing everything possible in 2012 to prevent Obama from a second term in office. That is politics.

> Humor is the virtue of allowing people to see your humanity and your comfort in being fully human, quirks and all.

But nations, like families, require moments of unity and tradition. Humor was brilliantly used by both presidents to humanize the occasion. Obama paid tribute to Bush, and then jokingly thanked him for leaving "a really good TV sports package" on the White House cable system. "I use it," Obama said. Bush, in turn, thanked Obama and then told the incumbent president that he could now look to his portrait from time to time and ask, "What would George do?"

Why the humor? What else could they do? Most leaders are spared anything that dramatic or awkward, but the principle remains the same. Humor is the virtue of allowing people to see your humanity and your comfort in being fully human, quirks and all.

Leaders know how to laugh with their team, with their people, with the public, and at themselves. Humor is a public admission that leaders are completely human, and that, in itself, is a virtue.

The Leader and the Media

The Medium Is Not the Message, You Are—and the Leader Must Know How to Deliver That Message

You are walking into your office, a bit distracted by what is on your mind. You turn the corner, where a camera is thrust in your face and a reporter lifts the microphone to your lips. What are you going to say?

Some leaders feel right at home with the media, while others break out in hives at the very thought of a media opportunity or command performance. But it really doesn't matter which kind of leader you are—if you are a leader, the media is part of your world.

By the midpoint of the twentieth century, the mass media dominated the cultural landscape. Leaders quickly discovered that the media owned and operated the only platforms capable of reaching mass audiences. And those audiences are huge, make no mistake. Even as the world makes its transition to digital media and away from paper and terrestrial broadcasting signals, the three main platforms of the so-called old media—television, radio, and print—represent realities no leader can ignore.

Furthermore, anyone who leads a large organization will encounter that moment when the phone rings and a reporter is on the other end of the line. Unless you want to set yourself up for disaster, you had better be ready to answer confidently, honestly, and in a way that you can live with for endless rebroadcasts. Leaders who lack skills in dealing with the media will find themselves in a moment of desperation that might end in embarrassment or worse.

Do I have your attention? Good. Because the average American home now has more access to news than the White House Situation Room had just a decade ago. There are so many television news departments, newspapers, radio stations, and magazines out there that, eventually, you can count on your organization or movement being the topic of some news interest.

But beyond this, you have a message you want to communicate. Even before that reporter comes looking for you, you need to gain a strategic grasp of how the media can help you get your message across to people far outside your own constituency.

> **Never apologize for having a message and for wanting that message to receive the widest possible coverage and exposure.**

Keep this firmly in mind: Never apologize for having a message and for wanting that message to receive the widest possible coverage and exposure. That is why you are leading. You are the steward of beliefs and convictions that your organization represents and to which you have committed your life. Your organization exists to serve the mission defined by those beliefs, and you have been charged to lead. So lead, and never apologize for leading.

Does an appearance on broadcast media scare you? Take advice from Roger Ailes, a communications genius who worked many years with President Ronald Reagan and then went on to make Fox News into a media powerhouse. Ailes, from whom I have learned much about the media, tells his clients that it all starts with a conversation, and you already know how to have a conversation.

"Good communication starts with good conversation," Ailes asserts. "If you converse well, then you should be able to transfer that ability to a lectern or TV or any other format." So what makes for a good conversation? Ailes gets right to the point—you have to be interesting.

The best conversationalists are those who are most interesting and who work at being even more interesting. Killers of interesting conversation include monotone and boring speech, dull and self-centered dialogue, monologues, jargon, and a simple lack of engagement with the subject. On television, a loss of eye contact with the camera or the program host is a killer. You have to work at being interesting on camera, even if your friends reassure you that you are interesting to them.

Here is one of the keys to all communication: People simply tune out the things that don't interest them. You know this is true. You remember how many teachers you tuned out in school because, bless their hearts, they were just not interesting. As a rule, interesting people engage in interesting conversation, but that rule is often broken by people who are lazy communicators. Your goal as a communicator is to not be tuned out.

Now add the context of the mass media. Your voice is competing with millions of other voices. Viewers can switch the channel with a flick of the remote control. In eras past, a speaker may have had time to slowly become interesting as the cameras rolled, but not anymore. Roger Ailes is bluntly honest. On television, you have seven seconds. By then viewers (and the program host) will have decided if you are interesting or not. If not, flick goes the remote control. Your message never gets out.

Newspapers and Print Media

I never expected to be a newspaper editor, but it happened. One of the most venerable Christian newspapers in the country elected me as editor at the ripe age of twenty-nine. Days later I found myself in Las Vegas, of all places, covering the 1989 meeting of the Southern Baptist Convention during one of the most controversial eras of the denomination's history. I had a good deal of writing experience prior to this appointment, but I had never been an accredited member of the press, much less the editor of a newspaper. I made a huge discovery in Las

Vegas—if you put a microphone in front of someone, they will talk and say the most amazing (and sometimes revealing) things.

Newspapers are making their way into digital formats, and the reassuring feel of newsprint in the reader's hand may not last much longer. But newspapers will continue to dominate hard news. They do so for one central reason—they employ the best reporters, writers, and editors in the business. That is not to say that television and radio reporters aren't gifted, but it is to stress that the level of editing at a major newspaper vastly exceeds that of most other media platforms. This is what gives newspapers their aura of authority as the "first run of history."

But newspapers, like all media, have to be interesting. Most are commercial enterprises that make the largest part of their revenue through selling advertisements. To make this worthwhile, the paper has to hold the reader's attention. If you want to get your message out through the newspaper, you must keep this in mind.

If you send out a press release, it had better be interesting. Don't expect an assignment editor to waste time on the boring or the ordinary. Meeting your institutional goals is not interesting except to you. Starting a new work for your organization on a just-discovered inhabited island is interesting, so lead with that. Don't bury your big news in institutional dressing; get to the point quickly.

If you want to get your message out through an op-ed column on the editorial pages, you had better have a good, clear point to make about an issue of very current concern, and your column had better be written well. Don't start by sending a column to the *New York Times*. Start local, start smaller, and work your way up the food chain. Contact the opinion editor of your local or regional newspaper and ask if there is an interest in your column. Make your case succinctly, or you are dead on arrival.

Never discount the power of the newspaper. As is true of both radio and television, we still live in a world dominated by the old triumvirate of mass media. More people will read your newspaper column than your blog, even if they read the newspaper online.

The same can be said of the magazine world. Look around at the local airport newsstand, and you continue to see print magazines staring you in the face. Sit down to wait at the doctor's office and the table is filled with magazines. The same rules generally apply to newspapers and magazines, though the magazines run on a longer print cycle.

One last word: The best way to learn what kinds of news items make their way into print and what kind of columns get printed on the opinion pages is to read those same papers and magazines regularly, carefully, and strategically. There is no substitute for familiarity.

Radio

America was transformed by radio in the early twentieth century, and it remains, even now, the most conversational medium among the big three. In fact, it has been reborn in recent years with a great deal of the nation's conversation migrating to the radio airwaves.

I grew up hearing radio legends like Paul Harvey read and interpret the news. Radio brought voices into America's homes and established a medium that would be exploited to the fullest by both politicians and preachers.

For eight years I had the honor of hosting a daily live national radio program. It was exhilarating, and I still miss it. There is nothing like the thrill of a live microphone and the knowledge that all that stands between the listener and dead air is your voice. I also loved engaging with listeners, especially those who called in to the program with comments and questions.

Radio is a medium in transformation. Almost no one buys a radio these days; they buy things (like cars) with radios in them. Keep in mind that the radio audience is largely a captive audience. People are in cars, in offices, in the kitchen, listening as they do their work or stare at the cars in front of them. So radio thrives by being the listener's companion and conversation partner.

You want to be a part of that conversation because you have a message you want to share with others. The main opportunity on radio is the interview. This includes the brief news interview or an appearance on a longer talk radio program. Both are important, and both require—no surprise—that you be interesting.

One additional word on radio: On the radio waves, you have one central asset—your voice. No one can see your facial expression or your gestures; all they have is your voice. You do not have to be James Earl Jones, but you do have to speak in a clear, expressive, responsive voice. Otherwise your message will be lost in the fog and the producer will cue the next ad. Be interesting and speak in an engaging tone and voice rhythm. Understand that radio hates dead air, so open your mouth and talk. Hesitation kills interest.

Television

If America was transformed by radio, it was transformed all over again by television. Television added the visual image to the mix and has been getting better at it all the time. Now the voice has a face and a body. Everything has changed.

You have a message, and you cannot ignore television. In terms of local television news, the rules are very similar to those of radio, except you must keep in mind that the audience is now reading your appearance, your dress, your facial expressions, and your gestures. The camera can be counted on to capture everything, so be prepared.

In terms of impact, nothing yet exceeds the nationally broadcast networks and cable news channels. I was a guest on CNN's *Larry King Live* dozens of times, going back almost twenty years, and I still hear from viewers about those programs. Larry King, by the way, is one of the world's greatest interviewers, and that is precisely because he is one of the world's most natural conversationalists.

I have also appeared on shows like *Good Morning America*; *The Today Show*; *Dateline NBC*; *PBS NewsHour;* the ABC, CBS, and NBC nightly news programs; as well as shows with hosts ranging from Chris Matthews to Bill O'Reilly. The constant is the fact that these shows have to be interesting and that they drive the national conversation.

If you want to get your message out on these platforms, learn to face a camera with confidence, learn to immediately lead with something interesting, learn to answer the interviewer's questions, and learn how to be warm and unflappable on the outside, even when you are frustrated and agitated on the inside. The camera reads emotions more quickly than the microphone carries words.

And, as Roger Ailes reminds us again, be conversational. By the way, Ailes was the producer of *The Mike Douglas Show* back in the golden age of the morning talk show. He developed a chart on which he rated guests for the program. The chart ranged from *boring* to *okay* to *interesting* to *memorable* to, finally, *book him back*. That chart pretty much says it all.

Finally, Ailes made this observation:

> What I've learned firsthand is that television has also changed the way we view each other. As a result of TV, people today expect to be made comfortable in every communications situation. When anyone speaks to them, they want to relax and listen just as they do when a TV professional entertains them in their living room.

To this he added, "You may think this is unfair, but that's just the way it is."

What to Do When a Reporter Calls

The phone rings, an email arrives, or a staff member walks in with a message. A reporter is on the line, in the lobby, or right behind your assistant. By then it is too late to decide how you will respond. Leaders need to determine in advance what to do when a reporter calls, because you never know when one will.

First, be honest. Never tell anything but the truth. You do not have to answer the question, and you certainly do not have to over-answer the question (a common mistake), but you can never lie, obfuscate, or fabricate. If you do, you will be humiliated, and you will bring disrepute on your organization and on the convictions you represent. For a Christian leader, this is inexcusable and injurious to the gospel. Furthermore, it is a practical disaster.

Second, be direct. Reporters are working on a news story or trying to find out if a story actually exists. Be up front with reporters and let them know that you will only answer what you can answer. Do not play games.

Third, realize that you can say no. You do not have to talk to every reporter who calls or take every media interview that is offered. I reject some programs, even very popular programs, because I do not believe that I can in good conscience appear on them. They would not allow the convictions I hold to get a fair presentation. I will not appear as a foil for someone else, and I do not enjoy appearing on programs that are little more than shouting matches. But if you do say no, just know that comes with a price. Even if you are right to decline, the price is that someone else tells the story, even when the story is about you.

Fourth, respect the reporter or program host. They are there to do a job, and you need them to do their job well. A reporter may appear to be hostile just because he or she has to ask a very direct question. If reporters asked you questions the way your grandmother would, they would never get their jobs done. On the other hand, if a reporter really is hostile, terminate the conversation respectfully. Radio and television hosts are professionals who bear the responsibility to manage the conversation on their program. Answer their questions and give them more than they ask for.

> Explaining what you believe is the very mission that brought you to this position of leadership.

Understand that time on air is measured in seconds and fractions of seconds. If you are interesting, concise, conversational, and warm, you will probably be invited back. Just think of Roger Ailes's chart.

Fifth, realize that reporters do not control the final form of a printed news story, and that radio and television reporters are also subject to editing. Don't blame the reporter at a major newspaper for the headline—she probably didn't write it. That is part of the editorial process. Don't blame the broadcast reporter for where your news story appears on the program—it's not his fault.

Sixth, realize that some media appearances don't go as you expect, and some don't even go. I have been in a studio hooked up for a live national interview with a camera on my face, only to have the entire segment canceled at the last minute because some Hollywood couple announced their divorce. That is the way the media work. And yes, as disappointing as it is, the producers really did think that the Hollywood divorce would be of more interest to Americans at that moment than the world-transforming issue I was there to discuss. Shake it off.

Seventh, know that everyone at every stage in this process operates out of his or her own worldview. It is a documented fact that those who lead the major media are more liberal and more secular, as a composite, than most Americans. Know that in advance, and understand that you cannot speak in Christian jargon if you want to be understood. Don't expect a secular news reporter to know what the Great Commission is. You will have to explain.

Eighth, building on what was just stated, know that explaining what you believe is the very mission that brought you to this position of leadership. That is what you live for, and that is why you have the conviction to lead. So go do it, and get your message out.

The Leader as Writer

The Written Word Remains One of the Most Powerful Ways to Lead, so Leaders Write

The invention of written language was one of the greatest human achievements, and the very fact that we can and do read messages written thousands of years ago is proof of its power. Leaders who want to make a difference, and to make that difference last, must write. You can write this down—leaders are writers.

William Zinsser, one of the most helpful modern guides to the act of writing, points to an odd and unpredicted development. We are shifting back again from oral communication to the written word. Teenagers (and now their parents) increasingly text each other rather than make a voice call. Email has now become the standard means of communication, displacing not only the printed letter but also meetings, phone calls, and oral discussion. We are all writing again. Not writing well, perhaps, but writing just the same.

The Leader Writes

There is no way to avoid written communication. Leaders generally receive and send a significant volume of written materials every day. Much of it is short-term and of little enduring value, but when matters central to the organization's mission and convictions are at stake, leaders must write with care and concern. Words matter.

Leaders must closely monitor their time and attention. There is no excuse for wasting time, but leaders often rush the wrong activities. One of those activities is writing. Leadership is about communication, and much of that communication is necessarily written, but far too many leaders undermine their leadership with poor writing.

Zinsser, who was a university professor in the 1960s, tells of the president of his university sending a letter to the campus that stated, "You are probably aware that we have been experiencing very considerable potentially explosive expressions of dissatisfaction on issues only partially related."

Seriously? As Zinsser explains, "He meant that students had been hassling them about different things." Now we understand.

In order to be understood, leaders must learn to write and to set time aside for writing. One important reason for this investment is the fact that the written word can do what the spoken word simply cannot do—sit flat on a page and demand attention. Most of the words we deploy in any given day can be forgotten almost instantly. But the words we want to last, to influence tomorrow and not just today, are words best committed to writing. Our only access to the ideas of the distant past are the written records that survive. This changed somewhat after the invention of recordings and the ability to preserve the human voice, but nothing has supplanted the book and other forms of the written word in terms of endurance, influence, and permanence.

Much of what the leader writes seems mandatory and mundane—such things as memos and notes and letters. Nevertheless, even these require clarity and have to follow rules of grammar and presentation. Furthermore, if these written communications are not important in their own right, there is no reason for the leader to spend time attending to them.

Leaders take words seriously because we live and die by them. We work to instill certain beliefs and convictions in other people and then to motivate and direct them to concerted action. This means that a memorandum on personnel policies is never just what it appears to be. Seen in the right light, it is a teaching instrument that should be maximized to affirm the organization's core beliefs and how those beliefs are now translated into the right set of personnel policies.

When the leader writes, he writes to inform, to motivate, to explain, and to inspire. Sometimes the leader has to clarify, correct, or even sound an alarm. Whatever the context, words matter, and the effective leader works hard to develop the ability to write clearly, cogently, and powerfully.

Learning to Write

The sad fact is that a student can graduate from high school and college and still demonstrate little writing ability. Few schools pay enough attention to writing, and some educational theories deny that writing standards should even exist. That is nonsense, of course, and the loss of the ability to write is a national tragedy.

The only way to become a better writer is to read and write as much as possible. No one makes this point better than novelist Stephen King. "If you want to be a writer," he asserts, "you must do two things above all others: read a lot and write a lot. There is no way around these two things that I'm aware of, no shortcut." Elsewhere, King says that reading "is the creative center of a writer's life."

Leaders who want to be writers, and thus to deepen and extend their influence, should identify writers and examples of writing that are particularly clear, effective, eloquent, and moving. Every writer has a personal style, but no writer is entirely self-made. The influence of many writers will show up in your own style, and sometimes that influence is considerable.

Again, as King said, learning to write starts with reading and then moves to writing. If you want to write, write a lot. The columnist whose style you admire probably started out as a beat reporter filing several stories a day, most of them long forgotten. The act of writing helps us learn how to make words work, how sentences come together, and how to make a message come through.

There are technical aspects, of course, and there is no shortage of classes devoted to the skill of writing. But few of the leaders whose writing you admire are themselves products of academic writing programs. They learned the craft by copious reading and voluminous writing, and you do not pay tuition for that kind of education.

The Leader and Words

All leaders lean into words; it just comes with the territory. For Christian leaders, the commitment to words is a matter of discipleship and personal devotion, for our faith is communicated by words. As John Piper has memorably said, we have to be willing to die for sentences. We even have to put ourselves on the line for single words.

Average leaders are satisfied to use average words in an average way. Effective leaders, those who aspire to lasting and extended influence, will learn to use words as arrows fired from a bow, carefully chosen and aimed in order to accomplish a purpose.

Mark Twain once said that the writer should aspire to "use the right word, not its second cousin." Sometimes this is merely a matter of style, but it can be a matter of meaning as well. By a careless use of language, leaders can end up miscommunicating or failing to say what they mean at all.

Leaders who would be writers collect words as they read. James Jackson Kilpatrick, a very clear and expressive writer, once explained, "If we would write well . . . we must collect words, store them, hoard them, fasten them into albums. They will be there when we need them."

How Writing Is Done

Leaders do a good bit of writing on the fly, composing a quick email or dictating a brief letter. I have dictated letters in the backseat of a

New York City taxi and I have written columns standing in a crowded airport terminal. You do what you have to do.

But if you are going to write seriously, and write for significance, you need a quiet place where you can devote yourself to writing. I appreciate Stephen King's candor when he says that the writer's most important equipment is a room with a door and the writer's determination to close that door.

Once the door is closed, get to writing. Most of us write on a computer these days, but there is still something to the experience of writing on paper with a pen, preferably a fountain pen. The flow of words in ink from pen to paper is uniquely satisfying. The computer, on the other hand, also offers numerous advantages for writing, allowing for editing, storage, and transmission with incredible ease. I must admit that I first found the experience of writing on a computer to be strange and awkward when I began writing in the early 1980s, but I soon realized that my productivity without the computer would simply not satisfy my needs, so I forced myself to learn to write on a screen. Now it is second nature.

John Updike once said there is no happier creature on earth "than a writer not writing." In other words, it takes effort to force yourself to write. You simply have to start and then let the words flow.

Roy Peter Clark helpfully suggests that writers should think of their readers as they write, and think of the process of writing as letting ideas and information flow from the writer to the reader. Clark urges writers to let the words flow before worrying too much about the rules and tools of the writing craft. Many writers never actually get anything written because they worry too much about the details. Write now, worry later.

> The written word matters longer and reaches farther than the words we speak.

Is writing hard? At times it surely is, but at other times the words simply flow and fall together. When you're working on a deadline, you have to get the writing done, regardless of whether it comes easily or hard. If you know in advance the times of day when writing comes easiest for you, plan accordingly. I write much better at night than in the morning. My mind is more alert and the thoughts and words flow more naturally. So I usually write at night (which is when I'm writing this chapter) and rarely write in the mornings.

Gather what you need and have your sources close at hand. Good writing is frustrated by interruptions, and the need for a source you do not have at hand is an interruption. Quiet is the friend of writers, but I write best with music in the background. I usually have classical music playing softly. The music adds rhythm and cadence to my writing. Oddly, I can often hear that music in my mind as I read my own manuscript.

> Good writing is frustrated by interruptions.

Once the piece is written, edit it. Make certain that it says what you want to say and with the style and tone you intended. If you are turning in a book manuscript or an article in a newspaper or magazine, a professional editor will improve your draft—at least in his or her judgment. If no professional editor will be involved, ask others to read your draft and comment on it.

Finally, turn in the manuscript and let it go. You will never be completely finished with it, and you will see things long after publication that you would change and say differently. Let it go. At some point Dostoyevsky had to stop writing and revising and finally turned *Crime and Punishment* over to his publisher. If he could relinquish his manuscript, so can we.

Writing as Leadership

Leaders write because words matter and because the written word matters longer and reaches farther than the words we speak. Leaders write newsletters, memos, correspondence, articles, columns, and books in order to extend their reach and deepen the impact of their leadership.

The conviction to lead means the conviction to write. If you cannot make this a priority now, set a goal for later. Collect words and examples of writing you admire, and develop the messages you want to communicate by writing.

While writing is demanding, its rewards are truly great. For inspiration, consider the words of legendary sports writer Red Smith: "Writing is easy. All you do is sit down at a typewriter and open a vein."

The Digital Leader

Leaders Understand That the Digital World Is a Real World—a World in Which They Are Called to Lead

The digital world did not exist a generation ago, and now it is a fundamental fact of life. The world spawned by the personal computer, the Internet, social media, and the smartphone now constitutes the greatest arena of public discussion and debate the world has ever known.

Leaders who talk about the *real* world as opposed to the *digital* world are making a mistake, a category error. While we are right to prioritize real face-to-face conversations and to find comfort and grounding in stable authorities like the printed book, the digital world is itself a *real* world, just real in a different way.

Real communication is happening in the digital world, on the web, and on the smartphone in your pocket. Real information is being shared and globally disseminated faster than ever before. Real conversations are taking place through voice and words and images, connecting people and conversations all over the world.

If the leader is not leading in the digital world, his leadership is, by definition, limited to those who also ignore or neglect that world. That population is shrinking every minute. The clock is ticking.

Peril and Promise in the Digital Kingdom

The digital world is driven by its entrepreneurial and ideological pioneers and cheerleaders, and they are a multitude. The numbers are staggering. The World Wide Web is, for all practical purposes, less than twenty years old. It now reaches every continent and country, linking over 2 billion people.

There are now 5.9 billion cellular subscribers, which is 87 percent of the world's population. Cell phones, originally the toys of the rich and powerful, are now more popular than landline phones in the poorest regions of the globe. The telephone pole will soon be an antique.

The blogosphere was unknown to humankind until fourteen years ago, but each month just one blogging platform (WordPress) logs over 300 million users who read more than 2.5 billion pages. The world now turns to Google before even thinking of reaching for a dictionary or encyclopedia. Most Americans under thirty cannot imagine a time when you had to go to a brick-and-mortar library for information.

Facebook, the central fixture of social media (for now), was launched in February 2004 and now links more than 900 million users worldwide. Twitter, the micro-blogging sensation, was launched in May 2006 and boasts 140 million users who post 340 million tweets each day. Even more amazing is the fact that more than 1.6 billion search queries are performed on Twitter a month. For many Americans, Twitter represents the leading edge of news and communication.

The digital kingdom is massive and transformative. Older media are migrating to the web, even as social media increasingly supplants voice technologies. Smartphones are primarily small computers, used occasionally for voice calls.

The digital world is the Wild West of information sharing and conversation. Just about anything can be found on the Internet, usually within a couple of mouse clicks. This includes everything from preaching to pornography, with politics and entertainment added to the mix.

While the Internet and digital technologies connect people, they also disconnect them. So much instant information and entertainment is available that it seems the entire globe is developing an attention deficit problem. At the same time, these technologies have led to the greatest democratization of communications since the advent of spoken language. Christians can take the gospel into China, leaping over the "Great Firewall," which is what Chinese citizens call the efforts of their government to keep information out.

> **The digital world is itself a *real* world, just real in a different way.**

North Korea struggles to isolate its people from the outside world, but cell phones (from Egypt!) are increasingly common, though illegal.

The Internet has also disrupted the stable hierarchies of the old information age. A teenager with a computer can create a blog that looks more authoritative than the blog written by a CEO of a Fortune 500 corporation—and perhaps read by more people as well.

Most of what appears on the Internet is unedited, and much of it is unhelpful. Some is even harmful. But we certainly cannot ignore it. If you are not present on the Internet, you simply do not exist, as far as anyone under thirty is concerned. These "digital natives" rarely receive and even more rarely write letters. They know nothing but instant information, and studies indicate that they multitask by instinct, utilizing several digital devices at once, often even while sitting in a classroom.

The digital world is huge and complicated and explosive. It contains wonders and horrors and everything in between. And it is one of the most important arenas of leadership our generation will ever experience. If you are satisfied to lead from the past, stay out of the digital world. If you want to influence the future, brace yourself and get in the fast lane.

Developing an Internet Presence

By now, just about every church, corporation, business, school, or organization has a presence on the Internet. If not, realize that you just do not exist, as far as untold millions of people are concerned. If you are a leader, you are responsible to see that your organization's Internet presence is useful, attractive, inviting, and well designed. If you need help, get help. The first impression you make on the web is often the only impression you'll get to make at all, so make sure it counts.

Content is king. People come to your website because they are looking for information. Make sure they can find it, and make certain it is worth finding. Your web presence advertises to the world who you are, what your organization is all about, and the seriousness of your commitment to that mission. The information on your site must be regularly updated and worthy of attention. If your Internet presence looks stale, visitors will assume that your organization is stale as well.

> You have a message to communicate, and there is absolutely no virtue in failing to communicate that message.

As leader, consider establishing your own Internet presence as a part of your organization's site. If this seems self-aggrandizing, recognize that this comes with the territory when you are a leader. Visitors want to know what you think, how you communicate your organization's mission, and whether you inspire trust.

You have a message to communicate, and there is absolutely no virtue in failing to communicate that message. Make your website serve the mission of your organization and drive visitors onto its pages. Offer good content, and visitors will come back. Let it grow old, and they will go elsewhere. This means a loss for your organization and its mission. Never forget that.

Make certain that visitors can find you and your organization. If search engines do not know you exist, only those who already know your Internet address can find you. That is not a growth strategy.

The Blogosphere

Not long ago, leaders found comfort in the thought that bloggers were all twentysomethings in pajamas writing online rants. That assumption has been blown out of the water by the fact that blogs, whether labeled as such or not, are now one of the most significant platforms for our cultural conversation. The White House hosts a daily blog, as does just about every major institution in the nation. The blogosphere, as it is now called, offers history's most cost-efficient way of communicating big ideas and solid content. If you are not writing a blog, you should be.

Some leaders write blogs meant for a huge international readership, others for mostly internal consumption. I started blogging as soon as I could find a platform, and I have worked at it steadily ever since. Although I write books and articles, speak all over the country, and appear in the media, nothing comes close to the reach of my blog. My books (I hope) will endure longer and communicate more deeply, but no book can broadcast ideas as quickly and inexpensively as a blog.

A blog requires constant feeding, and I have to keep it always in mind. At times I can feed it generously, but some days I have to let other priorities and opportunities reduce what I can do on the blog. If you do not enjoy writing, you will not be good at blogging. If you do, you should think carefully about what you are trying to accomplish. Most of my blog articles are large, and this is generally due to the magnitude of the issues I discuss. It does not have to be so. Leaders should let their blogs play to their strengths, but always make it clear, interesting, and serve the mission of your organization. In other words, blog with conviction.

Along the way, learn the tricks of the trade. Learn how to use links, images, and social media to drive people to your blog.

Social Media

The world's conversation is shifting fast toward social media, and this is now true for a spectrum of generations. Your grandparents might well be on Facebook and Twitter. As with the digital world as a whole, there are dangers and traps. Social media can be used for good or evil. It can connect people and it can disconnect them. But know this: Social media will soon dominate all other forms of digital communication.

That fact is reason enough for leaders to be engaged in social media. Facebook is now the fastest and easiest way to get to know a person—or at least to know how that person presents herself on Facebook. I use Facebook, but the limitations of Facebook for mass communication are frustrating. As long as Facebook limits individuals to five thousand "friends" on personal pages, it will be a frustration to leaders. On the other hand, you and your organization should have a Facebook "fan" page and learn to use it wisely.

Twitter is fast becoming the leading edge of social communication. I let Twitter feed my Facebook page, and I work hard to inform my constituencies and Twitter followers day by day. Twitter is now my first source for news. Tweets announce headlines, and I follow the links to the news stories. It is a huge time-saver and alert system.

A tweet may be limited to 140 characters, but users have brilliantly exploited that platform. The economy of characters is the charm, the most brilliant coercion of conciseness imaginable. If you are not on Twitter, and if you are not working and following it regularly, you are missing a massive leadership opportunity. Twitter, used wisely, can drive enormous traffic to your content, your organization, and your convictions. How can you justify leaving all that behind?

Podcasts and Streaming Media

The old media are tightly contained and controlled by large corporations or organizations. They have to be, given the vast costs associated with platforms based in radio, television, and print publications. The digital world opens the opportunity for you and your organization to become a producer of video and audio content without the massive investment.

Podcasts and streaming media allow you to do this, but they must be done well. This requires a significant investment of time and attention, and some investment of capital as well, but the ability to communicate by these technologies is powerful.

I present a daily podcast five days a week known as *The Briefing*, which is a review of the news from a Christian worldview. It is a huge undertaking, but it allows me to talk to many thousands of people each weekday morning. I can (and must) record that program from anywhere on the planet, and upload it to Louisville for production and release. Creating a podcast is a powerful opportunity for a leader, but you can start small. If it works for you, develop it.

My long-format program, *Thinking in Public*, is intended to be weekly and is between forty-five minutes and an hour. I interview a prominent public intellectual and engage with his or her thought. It is always lively, and I have been able to present conversations with people ranging from Alan Dershowitz of Harvard Law School to former president Jimmy Carter.

Your own podcasts could be used internally or shared with the larger world. Your program should fit your personality, your time, your interests, and the resources available to you. While your organization probably produces a significant amount of content already, much if it likely dies quickly. The use of streaming media allows content to be shared, and this is a good investment of institutional time and funds. Share the content with others, as long as it's worth sharing.

The Digital Leader: The Tools

A leader ready for influence and leadership in the digital kingdom needs, at the very least, access to the Internet and support for a presence there. You do not have to own a computer, but you do need one close at hand that is connected to the Internet.

At home in my study and at my office, I use a desktop computer with an oversized monitor. It allows me to work with at least two windows open at the same time, which is incredibly helpful for blogging, allowing me to write and research simultaneously. On the road I use a Macbook Air, which allows me to do just about anything I need to do (including, with a special microphone, my daily podcast), but I can still carry it easily.

A smartphone and an iPad make a leader's job easier. Indeed, the iPad has revolutionized the way I work, becoming more useful to me than a smartphone, especially for email and social media.

I am also a bold advocate for digital reading devices, such as the Amazon Kindle and the Barnes & Noble Nook. I own both and use both, and I also have their apps on my iPad. I am absolutely, unconditionally committed to the codex, the book printed on paper, but I am also a cheerleader for ebooks. Robert Darnton, the librarian of Harvard University, was recently a guest on my long-format program *Thinking in Public*. Darnton, responsible for the largest academic library in the world, affirmed that the printed book and the ebook are not enemies. I am in complete agreement. Some books will remain best read in print. Others can be read well as ebooks. Nothing can replace the feel of a printed book in your hands, but at the same time nothing can compete with the ability to carry a few hundred books at once.

Leaders are readers, whether in print or on a screen. And leaders belong in the digital world, leading with conviction. Leaders have a message, and should be ready to use every appropriate platform and technology to get it out to others.

The Leader and Time

Leaders Know That Time Is the Great Equalizer of Humanity

"Time is the scarcest resource," reminds Peter Drucker, "and unless it is managed, nothing else can be managed."

How is that for a depressing statement? Most leaders know that time is precious and that it is, in a sense, not on our side.

Human life has been transformed in recent decades. We have gained the ability to travel with remarkable ease. We have developed communication systems that put us in virtually instant reach of almost anyone in the world. We have revolutionized politics and science, economics and management. Nevertheless, time stands unchanged.

I find myself constantly humbled by the fact that I am limited to the same twenty-four-hour days that Abraham and Jacob knew. The scarcity of time is the great leveler of humanity, affecting the rich and the poor, the powerful and the powerless.

That is a hard lesson for all of us, and it was Drucker who helped me understand time in terms of leadership. I read his most important book, *The Effective Executive*, when I was a very young man. I found

> **The scarcity of time is the great leveler of humanity, affecting the rich and the poor, the powerful and the powerless.**

it humbling then and even more so today. To put it bluntly, I have much less time ahead of me now.

"Effective executives," Drucker insists, "do not start with their tasks. They start with their time." That is essential advice. Leaders understand that time is working against them, and that success or failure depends upon the right deployment and stewardship of time. Drucker also admonishes leaders to know that time is "totally irreplaceable." As he observes,

Within limits we can substitute one resource for another, copper for aluminum, for instance. We can substitute capital for human labor. We can use more knowledge or more brawn. But there is no substitute for time.

Convinced? Drucker is not finished.

Everything requires time. It is the only truly universal condition. All work takes place in time and uses up time. Yet most people take for granted this unique, irreplaceable, and necessary resource. Nothing else, perhaps, distinguishes effective executives as much as their tender loving care of time.

That last phrase caught my imagination decades ago, and I am still captivated by it. Leaders are distinguished by "their tender loving care of time."

But what does this mean? We can be humbled by the limitations of time without gaining any real wisdom in terms of its stewardship. Drucker advised leaders to carefully analyze where their time goes, convinced (rightly) that much of the executive's time was wasted on peripheral matters. Wisely, he also urged leaders to allocate significant discretionary time for the thinking and planning that are central to leadership.

But beyond this, in Drucker's book time is reduced to charts and graphs and analytical analysis. I do not doubt the value of that data, but Christian leaders are charged to think about our stewardship of time on very different terms.

The Backdrop of Eternity

The first thing we learn about time in the Bible is that God created it and that time is contrasted with eternity. Time characterizes creation, but the Creator is eternal. God is not bound by time, and he created time as a feature of the creation that reveals his glory.

This means that we must always understand time against the backdrop of eternity and God's eternal purposes. All of human history will be like the twinkling of an eye in the context of eternity, and every minute of time that we experience is a reminder of the distinction between God in his timelessness and us in our temporality.

The consciousness of time is at least part of what separates human beings from the animal kingdom. The beasts of the field and the birds of the air are bound by the same twenty-four-hour days we know, and they are also mortal, experiencing life between the two realities of birth and death. The difference is that we, unlike the animals, know the experience of time and its humbling reality. We look in the mirror and see its effects. We watch the days pass into months, the months into decades.

At the same time, even as we experience the time-boundedness of human experience, we also know that there has to be more. In the book of Ecclesiastes, we find a breathtakingly beautiful testimony to the meaning of time:

> For everything there is a season, and a time for every matter under heaven: a time to be born, and a time to die; a time to plant, and a time to pluck up what is planted; a time to kill, and a time to heal; a time to break down, and a time to build up; a time to weep, and a time to laugh; a time to mourn, and a time to dance; a time to cast away stones, and a time to gather stones together; a time to embrace, and a time to refrain from embracing; a time to seek, and a time to lose; a time to keep, and a time to cast away; a time to tear, and a time to sew; a time to keep silence, and a time to speak; a time to love, and a time to hate; a time for war, and a time for peace.
>
> Eccesiastes 3:1–8

Solomon declares the meaningfulness of time, but he then states that God "has put eternity into man's heart" (verse 11). In other words, we are captives of time, but we long for more. Furthermore, this knowledge of eternity affirms that our lives mean more than mere time can contain. Our earthly lives must be measured by an impact that is eternal rather than merely temporal.

This means, most importantly, that the Christian leader understands his calling in terms of God's eternal purposes and plan. The importance of this framework for thinking cannot be emphasized enough, and this puts the Christian leader into a completely different frame of mind than a leader who operates out of some other worldview. We, like all other leaders, are limited to the same twenty-four-hour day. But we are not limited to the horizon of earthly time. We want our lives to serve an eternal purpose.

The second truth the Christian leader knows is that our time is in God's hands. We did not choose when to be born, nor will we choose when we die. God made us for his glory and for a purpose within his plan. In the Sermon on the Mount, Jesus asked his disciples, "And which of you by being anxious can add a single hour to his span of life?" (Matthew 6:27). We cannot add time; we can only exercise stewardship over the time we are given.

The Christian leader knows that a day of judgment is coming, when every minute of our lives will be exposed to God's righteous judgment. That is a sobering thought, but it underlines the importance of our faithfulness in the stewardship of the time we are given.

The Tender Loving Care of Time

So how are we to exercise the faithful stewardship of time? The first task, as Peter Drucker reminds us, is to be honest about how we use it. Time-wasters, he advises, "abound in the life of every executive."

True enough. For the Christian leader, these might be even harder to identify and deal with honestly. Many have to do with the balance between availability and time away from others. Leaders have to be available, but no one can be available at all times. The effective leader learns how to be available at the right times—the times that will make the most difference.

The expectation of constant availability will defeat any leader and render leadership ineffective. At the same time, the essence of leadership is the transformation of conviction into corporate action, and this requires the leader to be available and present at just the right times—the times that reinforce that transfer of conviction into the mission of the organization.

Cultural trends can affect this balance, and I fear that many Christian leaders (including many pastors) have made themselves too unavailable. Leaders must protect time against constant interruption and distraction, but the people placed within their care and influence are not, in themselves, interruptions or distractions. No one said striking the right balance would be easy. The most effective leaders, however, learn to negotiate this balance by both insight and intuition.

Leadership by conviction affirms the reality that leadership is an intellectual enterprise. It is more than intellectual, of course, but never less. And intellectual work requires large blocks of uninterrupted time. Planning, strategy, conception, analysis, evaluation—all of these are intellectual activities. Add to these the task of framing messages and the ongoing responsibility to continue learning.

Knowledge of eternity affirms that our lives mean more than mere time can contain. Our earthly lives must be measured by an impact that is eternal rather than merely temporal.

Faithful leaders know that time has to be protected or it will be lost. Once lost, it can never be regained. This requires hard decisions and maturity. Followers rarely know what the burden of leadership requires, but they can and do sense whether or not the leader is ready when duty calls, confident in plan and purpose, and anchored in conviction and passionate about the mission. They may not understand everything the leader does with his time, but they will be able to tell if the leader stewards it well. The proof is in the quality of leadership, and the quality of leadership will determine the effectiveness of the entire organization.

⸗ Personal Time, Your Time

The leader's stewardship of time fits within the context of the leader's life and times. A friend of mine once observed that time moves much slower just after the birth of a child. The joys and instant burdens of parenthood displace many other priorities for a season. That big project at work will probably not get as much attention in the months just after a baby's birth. On the other end of the spectrum, my wife and I are now adjusting to the empty-nest syndrome. We are still hard-pressed for time, but in a very different season of life.

Most organizations follow some kind of annual rhythm. The church year and the school year slow down in summer months—not so if you're running an amusement park. Retail businesses know their peak seasons. The effective leader plans with all this in mind.

When I read Drucker's *The Effective Executive* as a young man, I was greatly influenced by his wise observation that some people are morning people and others are night people. I knew instantly where I fit on this continuum, and I have known this since I was in junior high school. This distinction is not so important in a world of physical labor, but it is fundamental in a world of intellectual work. Some of us do our best thinking in the morning, while others do better at night. As Drucker advised, lean into your strengths and compensate for your weaknesses. If circumstances demand that a morning person has to do intellectual work at night, he will have to work harder to produce the same results. The same works in reverse. When the leader has discretion, he should plan the stewardship of time so that strengths are maximized and weaknesses are minimized.

The faithful leader knows that time must be measured against the backdrop of God's eternal character and purposes. Everything humans build will one day be reduced to ruins, but our lives and our leadership will, in Christ, have eternal consequences and impact.

The faithful leader lives every minute within that frame, even as he measures months and years and decades in terms of stewardship. Day by day, the leader negotiates the challenge of time, and minute by minute he senses it passing. The leader knows a time to work and a time to rest, a time to plan and a time to act, a time to read and a time to speak, a time to play and a time to fight.

Long ago, I developed a habit of wearing a watch with an old-fashioned sweep second hand. I like to hear it tick, knowing that every tick marks the passing of time. I like noisy clocks in my study—clocks I can hear marking the time. I can feel the passing of time in my bones, and that knowledge makes me want to be a more faithful steward of time tomorrow than I was today. Time will tell.

Leadership That Endures

The Leader's Goal Is Not Only to Last but to Endure

We rightly admire things that last. That instinct is almost always right, especially when it comes to commitments and callings. We honor couples who have long and enduring marriages, and we recognize people for long terms of service. We may live in a culture of instant gratification and ever-shortening attention spans, but we still know enough to admire what endures.

This is especially true when it comes to leadership. The leaders who make the biggest difference are those with long tenure. Great impact requires a lengthy term of leadership, and the leader who wants to make a difference had better make a public commitment to stay.

Organizations are amazingly resistant to change. Even when change happens, it can be undone in a flash, as people return to old and entrenched habits of thinking and working. The most effective leaders know to stay on the job, determined to see the task done.

═ A Vision of Endurance ═

I saw this principle in action when, as a young minister, I visited the historic First Baptist Church of Dallas, Texas, for the first time. I wanted to experience the worship service and hear Dr. W. A. Criswell, the church's famed pastor, preach. The experience was memorable, to say the least. Criswell was one of the most famous preachers of the twentieth century, a master of biblical exposition and pulpit delivery. He was also a visionary leader who had led the church to become what was then one of the largest churches in the world. Furthermore, he was a titanic personality and a shaper of history. I wanted to see him in his prime, and he was. He was also almost eighty years old and still going strong.

Criswell had become pastor at First Baptist Church in 1944, following the death of the legendary George W. Truett. When I sat in the sanctuary on that day, Criswell had already been pastor there for over forty years. At the conclusion of the service, Dr. Criswell stood before the congregation and welcomed new members who had recently been baptized. One of them was a boy who was about twelve or thirteen years old. Criswell warmly embraced him and then faced the congregation and asked the boy's parents and paternal grandparents to come forward and stand with the boy. Then Criswell said something amazing. He introduced the boy's father, saying, "I baptized him many years ago." Then he introduced the grandfather and said, "And I baptized him even years before that."

This pastor had remained at his post long enough to have baptized three generations of men in a pastorate that spanned decades, and he wasn't done yet.

Just think of what that meant. Virtually everyone in that room had known only one man as pastor of the First Baptist Church of Dallas, Texas. George W. Truett had been dead for almost a half century. Criswell's imprint was on every square inch of that church's property, in every aspect of its ministry, and he loomed large in every living memory. More importantly, he had stayed long enough to reach deep into his congregation's hearts and minds. He had taught and preached and influenced successive generations—and his imprint is there still, now almost a decade after his own death.

As I sat in that sanctuary that sunny Sunday morning, I determined something that changed my life. I knew then that I wanted to serve in a place of leadership that would allow me—even require me—to stay for a lifetime of service and influence. I saw the glory of endurance right before my eyes, and I made the commitment at that very moment to aspire to know that glory in my own life.

> **If you want to make a lasting difference, you had better make the commitment to endure.**

Consider the alternative. Corporate CEOs, university presidents, and leaders of all sorts seem to come and go in a revolving door of forgettable leadership. Short terms for leaders are the rule rather than the exception. The average tenure of corporate leaders is amazingly short, and their leadership impact is frighteningly temporary. If you want to make a lasting difference, you had better make the commitment to endure. Otherwise, your influence will disappear about as fast as the stationery with your name on it.

Endurance, the Leader's True Patience

Patience is a virtue that is highly honored by Christians. The Bible reveals patience to be one of the fruits of the Holy Spirit. The apostle Paul prayed that the church would be "strengthened with all power, according to his glorious might, for all endurance and patience with joy" (Colossians 1:11). Evidently, patience and endurance and joy belong together. Paul also told Timothy to preach "with complete patience and teaching" (2 Timothy 4:2).

We often think of patience as a short-term issue. We are impatient in a checkout line, impatient in traffic, and horribly impatient as we sit on the tarmac at airports watching our time wasted by circumstances outside our control. More significantly, we are impatient with other people, often sinfully so. This is a major struggle in my own life, as I am often guilty of the sin of impatience about short-term things.

Without minimizing the sinfulness of impatience in that sense, a close look at the Bible reveals that the concern for patience is more often about the long-term endurance of a servant leader, willing and ready to bear the burdens of leadership and influence over a long time.

Observers of leadership have long noted that leaders often overestimate what can be accomplished in a single year, but underestimate what can be accomplished in a decade. That is a truly helpful word, and each of us has only so many decades in which to live. I will soon complete a second decade as president of the institution I am so privileged to lead. Each year I do a serious, gut-wrenching analysis of what we accomplished and experienced. Every one of these years has been eventful—some blazingly so—but I now have difficulty remembering what year a given event happened. Years blend into decades. To be honest, I never felt that a year was whole. On the other hand, the decades feel right. Years go by in a flash, but decades linger.

Three of my predecessors in office stayed for thirty-year terms. The history of this school, and of the churches we serve, demonstrates the massive influence left by those three men—influence felt even now.

Leadership Is an Endurance Test

Every branch of the United States military requires a physical endurance test as part of basic training. We can easily understand why. The armed services need to know, and know for certain, who can endure on the field of battle.

Leadership is an endurance test that will demand the best of anyone. Leaders face countless frustrations, mind-boggling complications, and pockets of resistance. It is lonely at the top, and the burdens of leadership can be demoralizing and wearying. Leaders know highs that are unbelievably high, followed by lows that are heartrendingly low.

Dr. Duke K. McCall, one of those leaders who preceded me in this office and served for over thirty years, once told me that institutions and organizations don't actually need a president every day. "But on the days a president is needed," he said, "it is because only the president can make the difference between success and failure."

That was an intentional overstatement, but there is more than a kernel of wisdom in it. Leaders should try to make a significant contribution every day, but some days are far more significant than others. Dr. McCall was elected president of our school in 1951, and he will soon be one hundred years old. He is a living repository of leadership, seasoned with an abundance of experience. When I was elected, Dr. McCall, already retired for more than a decade, told me that my job was to stay on the job longer than he had. He knows that I like a challenge.

Given the accelerating pace of corporate and institutional life, I am afraid that there are now more of those crisis days when the leader's decisive role is urgently needed, and the leader has to be ready at any moment for one to erupt. Endurance is what keeps the leader on the job, day in and day out.

Endurance is important for another reason as well. If you lead faithfully, you will make decisions that are unpopular, costly, and sometimes filled with risk. There are

> **Leaders have to bear the burden of right decisions that hurt.**

days when you will have to stand up and take the blame for a bad decision made by others, and plenty of other days when those bad decisions were made by you. But even more frequently, leaders have to bear the burden of right decisions that hurt.

Many years ago, sitting in a room filled with powerful executives and national leaders, I heard a prominent CEO make a statement in private that I have never forgotten. "Some days you just have to live with the fact that, if today is all there is, the folks who hired me would never hire me again. As a matter of fact, if today is all there is, I wouldn't hire myself."

Endurance not only makes demands of leaders, it also offers the blessing of a long memory and a longer period of evaluation. It takes time to see fruit grow on trees, and it usually takes even longer for the fruit of leadership to show itself in abundance.

A Long Obedience in the Same Direction

Eugene Peterson describes Christian perseverance as "a long obedience in the same direction." That is just about perfect. Holiness requires a long obedience in the same direction, staying on the field of battle and remaining there. The Christian life is often just a matter of simple obedience, putting one foot in front of the other and refusing to fall or falter.

The difficulty for most of us is the *long* part. We want everything to happen now. As Peterson explains, this impulse is deadly for the Christian life:

> Everyone is in a hurry. The persons whom I lead in worship, among whom I counsel, visit, pray, preach, and teach, want shortcuts. They want me to help them fill in the form that will get them instant credit (in eternity). They are impatient for results. They have adopted the lifestyle of a tourist and only want the high points. . . . The Christian life cannot mature under such conditions and in such ways.

Of course it can't. Neither can Christian leadership, for that matter. Leadership requires maturing, learning, adapting, rethinking, and retooling. None of these things come fast or easily.

Far too many leaders move from one position to another, over and over again, precisely because they do not want to endure the lessons that only time and tenure can teach. They jump from one position and land in another, building a long résumé but casting no shadow. They rob themselves and those they lead of the lessons gained only by perseverance and experience.

They prove the awful truth that you can serve in a leadership position and never really lead.

The Endurance of Truth

Convictional leaders prize endurance for one other fundamental reason—the endurance of truth. The truths we hold and the beliefs we cherish take the form of convictions that frame every aspect of reality.

Our mission is to see these convictions known, believed, and translated into meaningful combined action.

Truth is eternal, established by the God who is eternal. Those who know the conviction to lead must possess the commitment to stay and the ability to wait. The truth endures, and so must we.

The Leader and Death

Mortality Frames the Horizon of Leadership

"You're going to die. I'm going to die. It's going to happen." The Mohler family's favorite summer movie is *What About Bob?*, the comedy starring Bill Murray and Richard Dreyfuss. One of the most interesting characters in the movie is Siggy, an eleven-year-old boy named for his father's hero, Sigmund Freud. Siggy is incredibly thoughtful for an eleven-year-old, and at a crucial point in the movie, the boy—always dressed head to toe in black—reflects on the knowledge that he and everyone he loves is going to die. The bottom line is, "It's going to happen."

True enough. We are all going to die. Christians understand death to be the result of human sin and the final enemy that is defeated by Christ. But as long as this age continues, death comes to us all. The reality of death frames the urgency and importance of making the most of the time we are given.

Death is not our friend. The certainty of our mortality is a constant reminder that we are finite creatures who are truly living on borrowed time. Medical technologies and health can extend life for some, but death is an implacable foe. The cemeteries continue to fill.

What does this have to do with leadership? Everything. The stewardship of our time takes on an entirely new dimension. We lead with the knowledge that our time is limited, and that someone else will inevitably take over for us. As the old hymn reminds us, "Time, like an ever rolling stream, bears all its sons away." As most of us realize, that stream rolls quickly.

Awareness of our mortality changes everything. We know that our leadership, no matter our age, is a temporary stewardship. We are creatures made for a specific time and a specific opportunity and a unique stewardship of influence, life, and energy. This knowledge limits our pride and temptation to hubris, for we live with the constant awareness that everything we have built can be undone when we are gone. We have a limited opportunity to make a difference, and to make it last. Leadership, in other words, is perishable.

The desk I use for writing is clear of distractions except for one. A very realistic model of a human skull sits on the left corner. Some time ago, a visiting sixteen-year-old quietly advised me, "You have a leftover Halloween decoration on your desk."

Actually, it is not a Halloween decoration at all. If you look at some of the most historic portraits in the Christian tradition, you will see a skull within the painting. This was known as *memento mori*, the memory of death, which was intended to motivate the subject of the painting to make the most of the time given to him. That skull on my desk is not a morbid decoration or a macabre ornament from a dark holiday. It is a constant reminder of mortality as essential to the human condition, and an impetus to be aware that every passing day removes one tick from the column marked Future and adds one to the column marked Past.

If we had limitless time, we would lack any awareness of urgency. We would have no incentive to prioritize. Mortality not only is the great equalizer, it is the great motivator. Time and opportunities are precious and perishable. If we forget this, we lose all perspective. And perspective is essential to leadership.

You probably do not have a skull on your desk, but you had better have one in your imagination. From time to time I make my way to old cemeteries. One of my favorites is Princeton Cemetery in Princeton, New Jersey. I go there mainly to visit the tomb of Jonathan Edwards, one of my heroes. In the same cemetery lie the graves of famous Americans like President Grover Cleveland and infamous Americans like Aaron Burr. Added to these are the final resting places of numerous famous alumni and faculty from both Princeton University and Princeton Theological Seminary. Thousands of people pass by that cemetery every day without thinking about the people, no matter how famous or infamous, who are buried there. That is a humbling thought for any leader. There is no place as humbling as a cemetery—and there is no place more likely to remind the leader of the limits of one's leadership.

Most of these monuments are dedicated to the memory of someone we would identify as a leader. These individuals once ruled nations, governed states, or dominated scientific conversation. Now pigeons make their homes on these statues. No one remembers who these individuals were or what they accomplished. So is all lost?

The Leader Aims for Legacy

The knowledge of our own mortality would be devastating if all we knew was that we will lead for a season and then die. But turn this knowledge around, and it serves as the great incentive to aim for a legacy—the continuation of our influence and leadership after we are gone.

A legacy is what is left in the wake of a great leader. The leader is gone from the scene, but his influence remains essential to the direction and culture of the work he led. Once again, conviction is central. The idiosyncrasies of the leader will not (or should not) remain. The plans and visions of the leader will be outdated soon after his burial. The style of the leader is a personal signature. Your tastes will not be the tastes of the future. Yet none of this really matters. What matters is that the convictions survive.

Remember that leadership is conviction transformed into united action. If the convictions are right, the right actions will follow. The wise leader does not try to perpetuate matters of style and taste, or even plans and programs. The leader who aims at a legacy aims to perpetuate conviction. If the conviction is truly perpetuated, all the rest will follow. If the convictions are not perpetuated, none of the rest really matters. The leader who truly leads by conviction drives those convictions deep into the foundation of the movement. A legacy is built on that foundation as convictions frame reality.

> **Leadership is conviction transformed into united action. If the convictions are right, the right actions will follow.**

Charles de Gaulle was once told of an "indispensable man." De Gaulle quickly retorted, "The cemeteries are filled with indispensable men." They are, of course, and they hold indispensable women as well. Grave after grave of them.

In truth, there are no indispensable people, only indispensable convictions. The convictions came before us and will last when we are gone. Truth endures when nothing else can. This is the only real assurance that we have. Everything that we build and care for can be undone in short order. Eventually, every great achievement will fade. If all goes well, our successors will outperform us and reach heights we could only dream of.

This should be our hope, not our fear. If we are faithful stewards of the leadership entrusted to us, we will see ourselves as setting the stage for greater things to come. This was the determination of the patriarchs in the Old Testament. Abraham, Isaac, and Jacob all built for future generations. The great chapter on faith in the Bible's letter to the Hebrews records that Abraham, along with the other patriarchs, "died in faith, not having received the things promised, but having seen them and greeted them from afar" (11:13).

In other words, they led faithfully during their lifetimes and fulfilled their stewardship and then trusted that others—believing the same promises—would see these promises fulfilled by God. And they did see them, of course. The patriarchs and prophets of Israel define leadership by conviction, as do the apostles in the New Testament.

The knowledge of our limited time is crucially important. It is far too easy for a leader to believe his own publicity and to succumb to the idea that he is indispensable. If you're tempted in this way, just do as de Gaulle said and look at a cemetery to see the supposedly indispensable leaders buried there.

Years ago I heard the story of an old preacher who told a group of younger preachers to remember that they would die. "They are going to put you in a box," he said, "and put the box in the ground, and throw dirt on your face, and then go back to the church and eat potato salad."

That says it perfectly. Life goes on. If we transfer the convictions successfully, all will be well. If not, our stewardship is in danger . . . or in vain.

A Strategy for Perpetuating Conviction

Organizations develop strategies for what they value most. Strategies for growth, for profit, even for succession are demanded by most boards and expected by stakeholders. What is often missing is a strategy for perpetuating the very convictions that constitute the organization's basis for existence.

There are several strategic moves a leader can make that will greatly assist in perpetuating conviction. The first is to drive conviction into the genetic identity of the organization. Our own personal DNA shows up in every cell of our bodies, where it is replicated constantly. We must ensure that the convictions that frame the organization's identity are replicated in the same way—so pervasively that they become natural and expected.

Second, hire on the basis of conviction. This is essential, and yet this is where many leaders subvert their own leadership. We are all easily (and often rightly) impressed with expertise and ability, but these cannot compensate for a lack of conviction. When it comes to hiring leaders who will have a role in directing the work, conviction is nonnegotiable. You cannot possibly lead with conviction if you entrust the future of your organization to people who do not share those convictions. This is how great movements die—they begin with clarity and end with confusion, or worse.

Third, promote on the basis of conviction. How do individuals come to your attention for promotion? In any organization, there will be many different attributes and benchmarks that indicate progress and identify individual achievement. Furthermore, skilled leaders develop what can only be described as an intuition when it comes to identifying talent. Multiple issues must be considered when it comes to progress and promotion, but conviction had better be at the top of that list. It makes no sense to hire on the basis of conviction and then promote on some other ground.

> The loss of a secular institution is a shame. The loss of an institution founded on biblical truth is a tragedy.

Fourth, let convictional strength be the deciding factor in building your leadership team. Conviction cannot be tested on a meter, but it will be revealed in experience. Over time, you will come to know who stands with you in conviction and who does not. Build your core leadership team around those who share key convictions most intensely.

Fifth, document and communicate conviction everywhere you can. The key issue at this point is the perpetuation of conviction so that the truths you have given your life to serve stay at the heart of the organization, church, or institution. Ask yourself this question: What can I leave behind that will make the loss of these convictions less likely?

Finally, a word of warning. Just about everywhere you look you will see evidence of what happens when conviction is lost. Liberal denominations have been losing members for decades. Christians have established hundreds of colleges, universities, and schools only to see them turn and reject the very convictions that brought them into being. Even in the secular world, this pattern holds true. A study of the major philanthropic foundations in the United States found that very few of them remained in any sense connected to the convictions and concerns of those who originally funded them decades ago.

I am far more concerned with the loss of churches, denominations, colleges, seminaries, and other institutions based on Christian conviction and biblical truth. The loss of a secular institution is a shame. The loss of an institution founded on biblical truth is a tragedy.

Every leader needs to know the reality that we will die one day and that others will take our place. Hopefully, these new leaders will bring talents and abilities and vision greater than our own. Our greatest concern, however, is that they come with a wealth of conviction. Otherwise, all that we build can be turned against the very truths we have championed.

The Leader's Legacy

In the End, the Leader's Goal Is to Leave a Lasting Imprint

What will you leave behind? When all is said and done, what will remain when you are gone? The leader unconcerned about leaving a legacy is a leader who will leave the job undone.

No one stays forever. Leaders serve for some period of time, long or short, but the term of leadership always expires. That is one of the most humbling truths about leadership, and every leader must understand that whatever we contribute, build, and dream can be lost more quickly than we can imagine.

Without a legacy, our lives and leadership amount to little more than holding patterns in a world of decay. We should never discount the value of that holding pattern in a fallen world, and the lives reached and transformed by the mission we serve really do matter. But if it all comes crashing down when we leave, we didn't finish the job.

Rupert Murdoch is reported to have claimed that he aspires to no legacy. In the face of his critics, Murdoch said, "I'm not looking for a legacy." Then why is he leading News Corporation and his vast media empire? Is it just about the money and power? Is he truly unconcerned about what happens to his life's work? I doubt it.

The Perpetuation of Conviction

The leader's central concern with regard to legacy is the perpetuation of conviction. We lead because we are possessed by deep beliefs that mature into convictions. Our leadership consists of developing those convictions in others, who will then act together in the service of those beliefs, motivated to common action in the mission of sharing those convictions and living them out before the watching world.

If the leader's concern is merely financial gain and organizational aggrandizement, legacy will not matter much. This is what distinguishes convictional leaders from all others. The convictional leader strives to the end to see fundamental beliefs taken up by others, who will then join in the mission that grows out of those convictions.

The failure of leaders to develop a legacy is everywhere around us. Consider America's most historic and influential private colleges and universities. The vast majority of them were founded by deeply committed Christians for the purpose of educating young people in Christian truth. Within a stunningly short period of time, those schools, beginning with institutions like Harvard and Yale, abandoned their Christian commitments and established secular trajectories. James Tunstead Burtchaell calls this "the dying of the light," and he describes the process in which these schools abandoned their founding convictions, becoming openly hostile to the beliefs that called them into being. He writes,

> It was only later—usually about a generation later—that a new cadre of intellectuals, whose obedience was to a rational empiricism with no hint of bashfulness in the exercise of its articles of faith, transformed an institution whose original identity could no longer be confessed or asserted into a secularized academy.

Similarly, some of the most well-endowed charitable foundations in this country now function to subvert what their founding donors represented. It doesn't take long for that hostility to emerge. One of those founders, John D. Rockefeller Jr., explained the process in generational terms. The founder makes a great fortune, his children invest it, and his grandchildren squander it. There is abundant evidence that Rockefeller knew what he was talking about.

As we discussed in the previous chapter, the only antidote to that decline and fall is the perpetuation of conviction. Without the passing on of foundational beliefs, intact and in living color, those convictions will soon be eclipsed.

Succession

In any normal circumstance, the leader will be followed by a successor, who will inherit his or her stewardship. Looking around at an array of Christian institutions and ministries that have gone in radically different directions after the departure of a leader, a wise friend of mine quipped, "Well, when you are gone, you are really gone."

There is a great deal of truth in that. Gone means gone. The "emeritus" title, if granted, may mean very little. Once leadership is surrendered, there is little the departed leader can do.

The succession crisis in contemporary leadership is not limited to Christian ministries. The nation's largest and most influential corporations and institutions face similar challenges. The evidence indicates that most leaders are not very good at managing succession and most organizations do little more than hope for the best. Of course, hoping for the best is one way to ensure that the worst will happen. A faithful succession requires a great deal of planning and determination, and no successful model is applicable everywhere.

> The leader unconcerned about leaving a legacy is a leader who will leave the job undone.

Clearly, the leader's first task is to make certain that the organization's core commitments and convictions are shared by those who will hire the new leader. If the board does not share those convictions, it is highly unlikely that their chosen leader will hold the convictions with tenacity and passion. At a minimum, the leader's responsibility is to make certain that the board understands what is at stake. The board or committee may not take your advice, but they should have to reject it only by disregarding all that you have taught and modeled in your term of office.

Second, the leader bears the responsibility of building a leadership team of outstanding individuals who fully share the leader's convictions and vision. There is a huge difference between appointing those who are willing to sign on to those convictions and those who are eager to do so. In the language of our institutional contract, those who teach and lead here must affirm our convictions "without hesitation or mental reservation." Anyone with reservations should not serve in a leadership position. To allow this is to plant the seeds of your organization's destruction.

Third, the leader must communicate these convictions to the organization's various constituencies, laying a solid foundation for a healthy succession. In a healthy institution, the younger members are even more openly and deeply committed to the group's convictions than the older members are. Conversely, if this is not true, the organization can easily slide into convictional confusion or worse.

Fourth, the leader should strive to drive the convictions and beliefs so deeply into the culture and ethos of the organization that alteration or abandonment is seen as betrayal. For many Christian organizations, one key component of this accountability is a confession of faith or a statement of beliefs. Here at the Southern Baptist Theological Seminary and Boyce College, those who teach must sign the confession, pledging to teach "in accordance with and not contrary to all that is contained therein."

Fifth, this means that every hiring decision is a legacy decision. When we hire someone and put them into a position of leadership, they bring their convictions and influence as well. If those new people do not enthusiastically share the organization's convictions and beliefs, their lack of enthusiasm, if not their open antagonism, will weaken the work and threaten the mission.

Leadership succession is excruciatingly difficult because leadership is, by its very nature, so personal. I will not be succeeded by myself. Whoever follows me will have his own ideas, his own passions, and his own vision for the future. That is not only acceptable, it is necessary. The organization will need a new voice, will need to see with new eyes, and will need a new vision. The outgoing leader should celebrate these and get out of the way.

But the organization's foundational beliefs are a different matter. Convictional leaders cannot be satisfied to see those beliefs diminished, marginalized, or compromised. Insofar as we bear the stewardship to lead, we must indicate clearly and publicly that the continuity of conviction is essential.

I know that in writing these words I set myself up for a future confrontation with my own admonition, so I will make the case even more strongly. When my tenure of leadership is over, my responsibility will be to get out of the way and to celebrate the new vision, strategies, priorities, and plans my successor will develop. I will have to understand that my opportunity for establishing those realities is over.

But the convictions are another thing altogether. If my successor attempts to subvert the truths upon which this institution is established, I will do everything I can to stop that subversion in its tracks, even if it means haunting my successor from the grave, by memory.

The Scandal of Retirement

In the years after World War II, Americans developed the idea that the good life meant having a fulfilling career followed by a lengthy retirement. The ideal of retirement seems to be a life of leisure and ease, occasionally interrupted by travel and entertainment. That is a fundamentally dangerous concept.

In the first place, it is unprecedented in human history. The idea of a long period of unproductive leisure at the end of life is a modern invention, and it flies in the face of the Bible's exhortation to meaningful work and service for the kingdom. This retirement ideal is also financially irresponsible, since improved health and the extension of life—good things in themselves—have lengthened the typical span of life after retirement by many years. This is not economically viable for a large population over the long term.

This does not mean that we expect workers to stay in the same job until they drop of exhaustion, or that leaders must stay in positions of leadership until death. It does mean that the American ideal of retirement does not meet the Christian standard of faithfulness.

For Christians the issue should be redeployment rather than retirement. I dislike no part of the job I now hold, and I consider this leadership responsibility to be my life's calling, but I can envision a day when I am no longer president, when I do not have to sit in long meetings and bear the burdens of daily leadership. I can look forward, at some future point, to a time when I will not have to have a suitcase always packed, and when I can finally get to some of the writing and teaching projects that are important to me. I can certainly look forward to spending more time with my wife, Mary, who has so generously shared this leadership burden with me, and to investing more directly in certain lives and places where I might make a decisive difference. But all that is not retirement. It is redeployment.

> **The American ideal of retirement does not meet the Christian standard of faithfulness.**

John Piper puts this new vision of our lives into clear focus when he writes,

> Finishing life to the glory of Christ means resolutely resisting the typical American dream of retirement. It means being so satisfied with all that God promises to be for us in Christ that we are set free from the cravings that create so much emptiness and uselessness in retirement. Instead, knowing that we have an infinitely satisfying and everlasting inheritance in God just over the horizon of life makes us zealous in our few remaining years here to spend ourselves in the sacrifices of love, not the accumulation of comforts.

The Leader's Legacy

One of my distant relatives was named John Mohler Studebaker. He and his brothers moved to Indiana and started the Studebaker Wagon Corporation in 1852. They ended up in the automobile business, eventually creating a major automotive brand. John Mohler Studebaker became the president of that company, surviving until 1917. He could see that the automobile would supplant the horse and wagon, but he apparently did not grasp the scope of that great transformation.

The Studebaker line continued until the early 1960s, when the business collapsed, unable to compete with the bigger auto manufacturers like Ford and General Motors. The last car rolled off the assembly line in South Bend on December 20, 1963.

Several years ago I visited South Bend and went to see the Studebaker National Museum. It tells the story of the company well. There are Studebaker cars there, but there hasn't been a company making them for almost fifty years.

I noted my family name there in the history of that company and its eccentric place in automotive lore. There is sadness in the death of a company and in the loss of a founder's dream. But there were no tears shed in South Bend, for it really wasn't all that important. Just old cars.

But standing there I realized that I was determined to leave a legacy of conviction and a living organization, not just a museum to the glory of what once had been. The legacy I aspire to is the perpetuation of conviction and the furtherance of a worthy mission—nothing less.

Your legacy is all that remains when you are gone. Do you have any idea what that legacy will be? Answering that question honestly is part of what it means to have the conviction to lead.

Notes

Chapter 1: The Conviction to Lead

16   Sam Rayburn quoted in David Halberstam, *The Best and the Brightest* (New York: The Modern Library, 2001), 45.

18   Theodor W. Adorno, Else Frenkel-Brunswik, Daniel Levinson, and Nevitt Sanford, *The Authoritarian Personality* (New York: Harper & Row, 1950).

Chapter 2: Leading Is Believing

24   *St. Justin Martyr: The First and Second Apologies*, trans. Leslie William Barnard (New York: Paulist Press, 1996), 55.

24   Martin Luther quoted in Roland Herbert Bainton, *Here I Stand: A Life of Martin Luther* (Peabody, MA: Hendrickson, 2008), 182.

25   "I am commanded by the king to be brief": Robert Bolt, *A Man for All Seasons*, directed by Fred Zinnemann (Columbia Pictures, 1966).

Chapter 3: Convictional Intelligence

30   "one-dimensional view": Howard Gardner, *Multiple Intelligences: New Horizons*, rev. ed. (New York: Basic Books, 2006), 4. I do not accept anything close to Gardner's evolutionary worldview, but his idea of multiple intelligences does not depend on that worldview.

30   Daniel Goleman, "What Makes a Leader?", *Harvard Business Review*, June 1996, quoted in *HBR's 10 Must Reads on Leadership* (Boston: Harvard Business Review Press, 2011), 3.

Chapter 5: Leaders Understand Worldviews

43   "the silent shapers of our thoughts": Thomas Sowell, *A Conflict of Visions: The Ideological Origins of Political Struggles*, rev. ed. (New York: Basic Books, 1987, 2007), quote from 1987 preface.

44   "Visions may be moral": Ibid.

Notes

44   "We will do almost anything": Ibid.

49   Richard M. Weaver, *Ideas Have Consequences* (Chicago: University of Chicago Press, 1948).

Chapter 6: The Passion to Lead

55   Mario Vargas Llosa, *The Language of Passion*, trans. Natasha Wimmer (New York: Farrar, Straus and Giroux, 2003).

Chapter 7: Leaders Are Thinkers

65   "Bush: 'I'm the decider' on Rumsfeld," CNN, April 18, 2006, http://articles.cnn.com/2006-04-18/politics/rumsfeld_1_secretary-rumsfeld-military-personnel-fine-job?_s=PM:POLITICS ///.

Chapter 8: Leaders Are Teachers

67   Raj Chetty, John N. Friedman, and Jonah E. Rockoff, "The Long-Term Impacts of Teachers: Teacher Value-Added and Student Outcomes in Adulthood," National Bureau of Economic Research, December 2011, http://obs.rc.fas.harvard.edu/chetty/value_added.html.

68   David A. Garvin, "Building a Learning Organization," *Harvard Business Review* 71, no. 4 (July 1, 1993): 80.

Chapter 9: Leadership Is All About Character

75   Calvin Coolidge quoted in David Pietrusza, ed., *Silent Cal's Almanack: The Homespun Wit and Wisdom of Vermont's Calvin Coolidge* (Seattle: CreateSpace, 2008), 47.

77   "their idea of character was the outer life": Gordon S. Wood, *Revolutionary Characters: What Made the Founders Different* (New York: Penguin Books, 2006), 23–24.

77   "the current political debate . . . is literally destroying American politics": Richard Reeves, "John F. Kennedy," *Character Above All: Ten Presidents from FDR to George Bush*, ed. Robert A. Wilson (New York: Simon & Schuster, 1995), 92.

77   "In a president, character is everything": Peggy Noonan, "Ronald Reagan," *Character Above All: Ten Presidents from FDR to George Bush*, ed. Robert A. Wilson (New York: Simon & Schuster, 1995), 202.

78   "Character matters" and "We want character but without unyielding conviction": James Davison Hunter, *The Death of Character: Moral Education in an Age Without Good or Evil* (New York: Basic Books, 2000), xiii.

79   Stanley Hauerwas, *A Community of Character: Toward a Constructive Christian Social Ethic* (Notre Dame, IN: University of Notre Dame Press, 1981).

Chapter 10: Leadership and Credibility

84   "Leadership may once have been conferred by rank and privilege": James M. Kouzes and Barry Z. Posner, *Credibility: How Leaders Gain It and Lose It*, rev. ed. (San Francisco: Jossey-Bass, 1993, 2011), 2.

84   "a relationship between those who aspire to lead": Ibid.

Notes

Chapter 11: Leaders Are Communicators

92   "the difference between the lightning bug and the lightning": Mark Twain to George Bainton, October 15, 1888.

93   George McGovern quoted in Michael Leahy, "What Might Have Been," *The Washington Post*, February 20, 2005, 20.

Chapter 12: Leaders Are Readers

99   "Mary Higgins Clark," By the Book, *New York Times Sunday Book Review*, May 13, 2012, http://www.nytimes.com/2012/05/13/books/review/mary-higgins-clark-by-the-book.html.

103   "Naturally, since I myself am a writer": C. S. Lewis, "On the Reading of Old Books," introduction to *On the Incarnation*, rev. ed., by St. Athanasius (Crestwood, NY: St. Vladimir's Seminary Press, 1996), 4.

Chapter 14: Leaders Are Managers

116   "In less than 150 years": Peter Drucker, "Management and the World's Work," *Classic Drucker: From the Pages of Harvard Business Review* (Cambridge, MA: Harvard Business School Press, 2006), 181.

116   "Management has been the main agent": Ibid., 182.

116   "one of humanity's greatest inventions": Gary Hamel, *The Future of Management* (Cambridge, MA: Harvard Business School Press, 2007), 6.

117   "Managers are people who do things right": Warren Bennis and Burt Nanus, *Leaders: The Strategies for Taking Charge* (New York: Harper & Row, 1985), 21.

118   "to make people capable of joint performance": Peter Drucker, "Management and the World's Work," *Harvard Business Review* 66, no. 5: 65.

118   Drucker defines the work of the manager: Peter Drucker, *Management*, rev. ed. (New York: Collins, 2008), 8.

120   "the management theory industry": Adrian Wooldridge, *Masters of Management* (New York: Harper Business, 2011), 49.

Chapter 15: Leaders Are Speakers

124   "In the past all a king had to do": David Seidler, *The King's Speech*, directed by Tom Hooper (Weinstein Company, 2010).

124   "If I'm king": Ibid.

126   "I know I have the body but of a weak and feeble woman": Elizabeth I, "Speech to the Troops at Tilbury, 1588," *The Norton Anthology of English Literature*, 6th ed., ed. M. H. Abrams (New York: W. W. Norton & Company, 1993), 1:999.

126   "mobilized the English language": Winstonchurchill.org, "Quotes FAQ," last modified March 01, 2009, http://www.winstonchurchill.org/learn/speeches/quotations/quotes-faq.

126   "I had the luck": Winston Churchill quoted in Winston S. Churchill (grandson), *Never Give In! The Best of Winston Churchill's Speeches* (New York: Hyperion, 2003), 490.

131   Muriel Humphrey quoted in James C. Humes, *Speak Like Churchill, Stand Like Lincoln: 21 Powerful Secrets of History's Greatest Speakers* (Roseville, CA: Prima Publishing, 2002), 38.

Chapter 16: Leadership as Stewardship

134   "We have turned to a God that we can use": David F. Wells, *God in the Wasteland: The Reality of Truth in a World of Fading Dreams* (Grand Rapids, MI: Eerdmans, 1994), 114.

Chapter 17: The Leader as Decision Maker

144   Max De Pree, *Leadership Is an Art* (New York: Currency, 2004), 11.

146   Field Marshal Alanbrooke quoted in William Manchester, *The Last Lion: Winston Spencer Churchill, Visions of Glory* (New York: Little, Brown, 1983), 19.

146   "zigzag streak of lightning in the brain": Ibid.

147   F. E. Smith quoted in Ibid., 20.

147   "Whatever the verdict": George W. Bush, *Decision Points* (New York: Crown Publishers, 2010), 477.

Chapter 18: The Moral Virtues of Leadership

150   "He's arguably the greatest con of all time": Steve Fishman, "Bernie Madoff, Free at Last," *New York Magazine*, June 6, 2010, http://nymag.com/news/crime law/66468/.

151   "like great hunks of bleeding meat": William Manchester, *The Last Lion: Winston Spencer Churchill, Visions of Glory* (New York: Little, Brown, 1983), 4.

151   "heroic visions of what they were": Winston Churchill quoted in Ibid.

154   As told in a 1943 UP news story, quoted in Charles M. Province, *The Unknown Patton* (New York: Random House Value Publishing, 1988), 8–9.

155   Barack Obama quoted in David Jackson, "Obama Unveils Portrait of Bush," The Oval, *USAToday*, May 31, 2012, http://content.usatoday.com/communities/theoval /post/2012/05/obama-unveils-portrait-of-bush/1.

155   George W. Bush quoted in Tom Cohen, "Three Presidents Gather for Bush Portrait Unveiling," CNN Politics, May 31, 2012, http://articles.cnn.com/2012-05-31/politics /politics_bush-portrait_1_official-portrait-bush-family-bush-portrait/2?_s=PM :POLITICS.

Chapter 19: The Leader and the Media

158–159   "Good communication starts with good conversation": Roger Ailes with Jon Kraushar, *You Are the Message* (New York: Doubleday, 1988), 10.

163   "What I've learned firsthand" and "You may think this is unfair": Ibid., 15.

165   media are more liberal: Fred Barnes, "Liberal Media Evidence," *The Weekly Standard* (blog), May 28, 2004, http://www.weeklystandard.com/Content/Public/Articles /000/000/004/143lkblo.asp.

Chapter 20: The Leader as Writer

167   shift from oral communication to the written word: William Zinsser, *On Writing Well*, 6th ed. (New York: Quill/HarperResource, 2001), xi.

168   university professor anecdote: Ibid., 8.

169   "If you want to be a writer": Stephen King, *On Writing: 10th Anniversary Edition: A Memoir of the Craft* (New York: Scribner, 2010), 139.

169   reading as "creative center of a writer's life": Ibid., 142.

170 "use the right word": Mark Twain, "Fenimore Cooper's Literary Offenses," in *Great Short Works of Mark Twain*, ed. Justin Kaplan (New York: HarperCollins, 2004), 171.

170 "If we would write well": James J. Kilpatrick, *The Writer's Art* (Kansas City: Andrews McMeel, 1984), 44.

171 importance of a closed door: King, *On Writing*, 51.

171 John Updike quoted in Dinitia Smith, "Mansion Full of Honors in the Arts," *New York Times*, May 22, 1997, http://www.nytimes.com/1997/05/22/arts/mansion-full -of-honors-in-the-arts.html.

171 Roy Peter Clark, *Writing Tools: 50 Essential Strategies for Every Writer* (New York: Little, Brown, 2006).

173 Red Smith quoted in Ibid., 3.

Chapter 21: The Digital Leader

176 World Wide Web links 2 billion people: Jonathan Lynn, "Internet Users to Exceed 2 Billion This Year," Reuters, October 19, 2010, http://www.reuters.com/ article/2010/10/19/us-telecoms-internet-idUSTRE69I24720101019.

176 5.9 billion cellular subscribers: "Global Mobile Statistics 2012 Part A: Mobile Subscribers; Handset Market Share; Mobile Operators," mobiThinking, June 2012, http:// mobithinking.com/mobile-marketing-tools/latest-mobile-stats/a#subscribers.

176 Wordpress data: "Wordpress Stats," WordPress.com, accessed August 7, 2012, http://en.wordpress.com/stats/.

176 Facebook data: David Goldman, "Facebook Tops 900 Million Users," CNN Money, April 23, 2012, http://money.cnn.com/2012/04/23/technology/facebook-q1/index .htm.

176 140 million Twitter users and 340 million tweets per day: "Twitter Turns Six," Twitter blog, March 21, 2012, http://blog.twitter.com/2012/03/twitter-turns-six .html.

176 1.6 billion Twitter search queries per month: "Awareness, Inc. Unveils Industry's First and Only Social Scoring Capability That Drives Repeatable & Predictable Social Marketing ROI," Market Watch, *Wall Street Journal*, August 6, 2012, http://www.market watch.com/story/awareness-inc-unveils-industrys-first-and-only-social-scoring -capability-that-drives-repeatable-predictable-social-marketing-roi-2012-08-06.

Chapter 22: The Leader and Time

183 "Time is the scarcest resource": Peter Drucker, *The Effective Executive: The Definitive Guide to Getting the Right Things Done* (New York: HarperBusiness, 2006), 51.

184 "Effective executives": Ibid., 25.

184 "Within limits we can substitute one resource for another": Ibid., 26.

184 "Everything requires time": Ibid.

186 Time-wasters "abound in the life of every executive": Ibid., 28.

Chapter 23: Leadership That Endures

196 "a long obedience": Eugene Peterson, *A Long Obedience in the Same Direction: Discipleship in an Instant Society* (Downers Grove, IL: InterVarsity Press, 1980). Interestingly, Peterson borrows and adapts the phrase from none other than Friedrich Nietzsche.

Notes

196   "Everyone is in a hurry": Eugene Peterson, *Perseverance: A Long Obedience in the Same Direction* (Downers Grove, IL: InterVarsity Press, 1996), 136.

Chapter 24: The Leader and Death

199   "You're going to die": Tom Schulman, *What About Bob?*, directed by Frank Oz (Touchstone Pictures, 1991).
200   "Time, like an ever rolling stream": Isaac Watts, "O God Our Help in Ages Past," 1719, public domain.
202   "The cemetaries are filled with indispensable men": Sometimes attributed to Georges Clemenceau.
204   philanthropic foundations no longer connected to founders' convictions: Inderjeet Parmer, *Foundations of the American Century: The Ford, Carnegie, and Rockefeller Foundations in the Rise of American Power* (New York: Columbia University Press, 2012).

Chapter 25: The Leader's Legacy

208   "It was only later": James Tunstead Burtchaell, "The Decline and Fall of the Christian College," *First Things*, April 1991, http://www.firstthings.com/article/2007/10/002-the-decline-and-fall-of-the-christian-college-30.
209   See Ron Chernow, *Titan: The Life of John D. Rockefeller, Sr.* (New York: Random House, 1998) for more insight into the life of Rockefeller.
212   "Finishing life to the glory of Christ": John Piper, *Rethinking Retirement: Finishing Life for the Glory of Christ* (Wheaton, IL: Crossway Books, 2008), 6.

Dr. R. Albert Mohler Jr. serves as president of the Southern Baptist Theological Seminary—the flagship school of the Southern Baptist Convention and one of the largest seminaries in the world. Dr. Mohler has been recognized by such influential publications as *Time* and *Christianity Today* as a leader among American evangelicals. In fact, Time.com called him the "reigning intellectual of the evangelical movement in the U.S."

In addition to his presidential duties, Dr. Mohler hosts two programs: *The Briefing*, a daily analysis of news and events from a Christian worldview; and *Thinking in Public*, a series of conversations with the day's leading thinkers. He also writes a popular blog and a regular commentary on moral, cultural, and theological issues. All of these can be accessed through Dr. Mohler's website, www.AlbertMohler.com.

Widely sought as a columnist and commentator, Dr. Mohler has been quoted in the nation's leading newspapers, including the *New York Times*, *Wall Street Journal*, *USA Today*, *Washington Post*, *Atlanta Journal/Constitution* and the *Dallas Morning News*. He has also appeared on such national news programs as CNN's *Larry King Live*, NBC's *Today Show*, *Dateline NBC*, ABC's *Good Morning America*, *NewsHour with Jim Lehrer* on PBS, MSNBC's *Scarborough Country*, and Fox's *The O'Reilly Factor*.

Dr. Mohler is a theologian and an ordained minister, having served as pastor and staff minister of several Southern Baptist churches. He holds a Master of Divinity degree and the Doctor of Philosophy (in systematic and historical theology) from Southern Seminary. He has pursued additional study at the St. Meinrad School of Theology and has done research at the University of Oxford (England). A leader within the Southern Baptist Convention, Dr. Mohler has served in several offices including a term as chairman of the SBC Committee on Resolutions, which is responsible for the denomination's official statements on moral and doctrinal issues.

He is the author of several books, including *Culture Shift: Engaging Current Issues With Timeless Truth* (Multnomah); *Desire & Deceit: The Real Cost of the New Sexual Tolerance* (Multnomah); *Atheism Remix: A Christian Confronts the New Atheists* (Crossway); *He Is Not Silent: Preaching in a Postmodern World* (Moody); *The Disappearance of God: Dangerous Beliefs in the New Spiritual Openness* (Multnomah); and *Words From the Fire: Hearing the Voice of God in the Ten Commandments* (Moody).

Dr. Mohler lives in Louisville, Kentucky, with his wife, Mary. They have two children, Katie and Christopher.